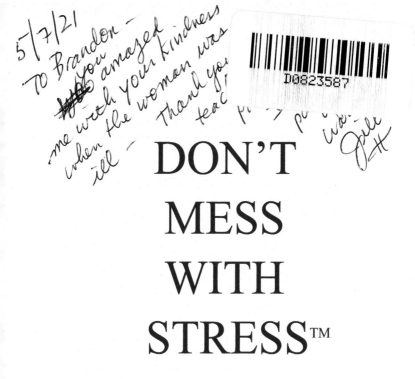

DON'T MESS WITH STRESS™

A SIMPLE GUIDE TO MANAGING STRESS,
OPTIMIZING HEALTH, AND MAKING
THE WORLD A BETTER PLACE

JILL R. BARON, MD

Printed in the United States of America
First Printing, 2020

Print ISBN: 978-1-7360244-0-9
Jill R. Baron, M.D., P.C.
Cover design by Jobelle Rosean Fortun

www.drjillbaron.com
Dr. Baron is available for speaking engagements. Please contact her through her website.

To Mom and Dad, with gratitude
for all your wisdom and support. You've always been
there for me. I love you so much!

CONTENTS

INTRODUCTION

THE AGE OF STRESS   1

OUR COMMON GOALS   2

ACCENTUATE THE POSITIVE   3

MY PATH AS A PHYSICIAN   4

GETTING TO KNOW YOU   6

DON'T MESS WITH STRESS™ (DMWS)   7

MY PATH AS A HUMAN BEING   9

BORN TO BE STRESSED   11

A TURNING POINT   13

IS STRESS INEVITABLE?   14

WALKING ON COALS   16

THE TRIUMPH OF THE HUMAN SPIRIT   16

CHAPTER 1: DIET, STRESS, AND YOU

BUILDING RESILIENCE   19

THE SKINNY ON PROCESSED FOODS   23

THE OPTIMAL STRESS-REDUCING DIET   25

NUTRIENT-DENSE FOODS   27

WATER   31

SUPPLEMENTS SHOWN TO REDUCE STRESS   32

DIET AND YOUR GUT   36

Prebiotics, Probiotics, and Your Gut   37

Alcohol and Stress   39

Create a Healthful Kitchen Environment   41

Eating Hygiene   42

The Buzz About Caffeine   44

Genetically Modified Organisms (GMO)   45

Non-Nutritive Sweeteners   46

Healthy Comfort Food   47

Food Sensitivities and the

    Elimination Diet   48

The Best Times to Eat   49

Onward   50

Chapter 2: Meditation

What Can Meditation Do for Me?   55

The Benefits of Meditation   57

My Path to Meditation   58

How to Choose a Meditation Technique   61

Let's Get Started   62

Introducing Meditation   64

A Meditation Journal   66

Final Thoughts   68

Chapter 3: Walk and Other

Forms of Exercise

Exercise: Super Stress Reducer   71

GENERAL BENEFITS OF EXERCISE 72

TYPE, DURATION, AND INTENSITY 74

WALKING AS THE CORE OF YOUR WORKOUT 76

THE 10,000 STEPS PER DAY "RULE" 77

STEP UP YOUR EXERCISE 78

YOUR TARGET HEART RATE 79

DANCE TO MAKE EXERCISE FUN 81

STARTING YOUR EXERCISE PROGRAM 82

THE DON'T MESS WITH STRESS™ DANCE 85

CHAPTER 4: THE QUEST FOR A GOOD NIGHT'S SLEEP

SLEEP, YOU, AND THE HUMAN RACE 89

YOU ARE NOT ALONE 90

WHY IS SLEEP SO IMPORTANT? 92

THE HAZARDS OF SLEEP DEPRIVATION 93

WHAT CAUSES INSOMNIA? 94

IMPROVING YOUR SLEEP HYGIENE 96

PROBLEMS FALLING ASLEEP OR FALLING

   BACK TO SLEEP 100

MEDICATIONS, TEAS, AND SUPPLEMENTS FOR

   ANXIETY AND INSOMNIA 102

ONLINE SLEEP RESOURCES 108

A GOOD NIGHT'S SLEEP IS IN YOUR FUTURE 109

CHAPTER 5: GAIN CONTROL OF YOUR MIND

BUILDING ON DON'T MESS WITH STRESS™

(DMWS)   113

SHORING UP YOUR MENTAL AND

EMOTIONAL RESILIENCE   115

A POSITIVE MINDSET   116

FINDING PURPOSE AND MEANING   117

HUMOR   118

SOCIAL CONNECTIONS AND NOURISHING

RELATIONSHIPS   120

HAVING COMPASSION FOR YOURSELF

AND OTHERS   121

"IN THE MOMENT" TECHNIQUES TO

MANAGE YOUR STRESS   124

ACKNOWLEDGMENTS   131

INTRODUCTION

THE AGE OF STRESS

EVEN BEFORE THE CURRENT CHALLENGES of the Pandemic, we lived in the Age of Stress. Life is so fast paced, we often can't catch our breath. Our hearts race, our stomachs are tied in knots, our mouths are dry and our palms clammy—these are all part of the brain and body's response to situations perceived as threatening. These symptoms are part of the "fight or flight" or "stress" response, which is activated by the **sympathetic nervous system**.

Think of the sympathetic nervous system as the stress response, and the **parasympathetic nervous system** as the peace response.

Everyone has personal stressors that trigger this stress

response: deadlines, traffic jams, a screaming child or a shouting client. Beyond that, we face the devastating, unpredictable events life throws our way, such as job loss, divorce, the death of a loved one. Then there is the state of the world to worry about. Will the Pandemic ever end? What about our children and grandchildren's futures? We are bombarded with news stories about environmental catastrophe or terrorism and other uncomfortable social and economic realities. At times these worries overwhelm us by day and make it harder to sleep at night. It's a wonder we make it through the week, much less a lifetime.

OUR COMMON GOALS

As a human being, a woman, and a doctor, I have special insights into the stresses you encounter in life. In my three decades as a practicing physician in New York City, I am all too familiar with the symptoms. I have witnessed how stress drains and damages the body and soul over time. I see it in my patients' faces, in their bodies, in their lab tests and EKG results. I hear it in their panicked reports of memory loss and requests for treatment for alcohol and substance abuse. Few are immune, whether they be Wall Street executives, frazzled single mothers, or affluent women who don't have to work. I have felt stress's impact on my own mind and body as I endeavor to help sick people and live a good and fulfilling life while negotiating the convoluted demands of the current American medical system.

ACCENTUATE THE POSITIVE

Our response to stress need not be deadly. It is true that stress can wreak havoc on the brain, the body, the telomeres that maintain the integrity of the chromosomes, the organ systems, and the immune system. It makes us more susceptible to disease, and it shortens our lives. But dwelling on our past failures to manage our stress gets us nowhere. **It is never too late!** We can undo a lifetime of worry and negativity by taking positive steps toward spiritual and physical wellness. No one can scare you into pursuing a healthier path; fear is not a sufficient motivation.

> Repeat after me: I am on a lifetime journey to learn how to manage my stress. Each step contributes toward my becoming a healthier, happier person. I will radiate that happiness back into the world and help show the way of health to others, transforming my stress-induced reactivity and anxiety into a power for good.

My goal for you in writing this book is to make

this affirmation a reality. There will be missteps and adjustments, backsliding, and setbacks, but with every positive step you make to heal yourself, you will come to discover that your resilience has no limits.

MY PATH AS A PHYSICIAN

I wasn't many years into my medical practice when I realized I needed a new approach: new insights and coping skills, both for myself and my patients. **Building physical and psychological resilience** in the face of life's stressors would be key.

I delved into both Eastern and Western traditions in nutrition, exercise, psychology, and spirituality. I read scientific studies, went to conferences and retreats, and sought out teachers, including Maharishi Mahesh Yogi, "Sri Sri" Ravi Shankar, Tony Robbins, and Nan Lu, OMD. Deepak Chopra, MD invited me to experience Ayurvedic Panchakarma, or purification, at a Transcendental Meditation® (TM) retreat center in Massachusetts, which opened my eyes to other possibilities for healing. I tried many techniques for managing stress and anxiety: meditation—TM and mindfulness; HeartMath®, Cognitive Behavioral Therapy (CBT), Psychotherapy, Dialectical Behavioral Therapy (DBT), Landmark Education, the Hoffman Process, and Art of Living Meditation. I also took courses in vitamins and supplements, nutrition, Botanical Medicine, Mind-Body

Medicine for Health Professionals, and in the new field of Functional Medicine, started by Dr. Jeffrey Bland. These trainings and therapies have all contributed to my ability to manage my own stress, empathize with yours, and help you discover your own path to a low-stress life.

I wanted to practice a different kind of health care, one that would combine paying attention to the body with attention to the mind and spirit—in other words, a holistic approach, one dismissed by many doctors at the time. I was tired of seeing up to 25 patients a day and not having nearly enough time to minister to them, of being stressed at running behind and making them wait. I was physically and emotionally depleted, suffering from the severe stress brought on by driving the 50-minute reverse commute to my job, feeling the pressure to see more patients in a shorter period of time—all this compounded by my fearful anticipation of confronting them after they had waited hours to see me. I began to have chest pain and palpitations. I was chronically stressed. I even developed a breast mass (which later turned out to be benign). The uncertainty of not knowing if it was benign added to my stress and anxiety until it was removed. I ended up selling my car and commuting by train.

In terms of my own stress management, I started meditating on the train to and from work, but it wasn't enough to decrease my stress. I needed psychological coping skills in the form of a mindset, philosophy, positive self-talk, and tools with which to approach my life and my work. I also needed to re-evaluate whether this job was worth the consequences to my health and well-being. Though many people in my life questioned why I would give up such a well-compensated position, I resigned from the group practice I was in with the goal of starting my own practice in Integrative Medicine. I would take the time to see patients in an unhurried and thoughtful manner and preserve my own health in the process. Later on, I would get certified in Functional Medicine, which is a form of Integrative Medicine that focuses on the root cause and the interconnections between mind, body, and lifestyle.

GETTING TO KNOW YOU

From the first, I knew I wanted to *talk* much more with patients. I asked questions doctors had never asked me and I had never asked of patients—questions about work, relationships, and the matters that worried them. I sat and *listened* to what they said—and what they didn't say or indicated only by their tone of voice or body language. In addition to writing fewer prescriptions and dispensing traditional medical advice, I began sharing suggestions about elimination and anti-inflammatory diets, home environmental testing, evaluations of their stool and urine to look for increased permeability and/or an abnormal bacterial balance in their intestines as a cause of their medical issues. The gratifying result: patients told me they felt their physical and mental state had been truly understood. They felt more cared for, less stressed, happier, and healthier, whatever their challenges. And they sent their friends and relatives to me.

In my history taking, I asked patients to tell me about the level of stress in their lives and the causes. Then, combining my investigations of the scientific literature concerning alternative practices, I recommended proven techniques such as Transcendental Meditation and Mindfulness, as well as Cognitive Behavioral Therapy and Dialectical Behavioral Therapy to keep ordinary stressors from triggering anxiety and for making inevitably stressful periods more bearable.

How Don't Mess With Stress™ (DMWS) Was Born

Having witnessed the harmful effects of stress on myself and my patients, I knew there had to be a way to deal with stress effectively with the least damage to our minds and bodies. I thought about what had worked for me or helped me over the years—a combination of lifestyle practices, physiological "In The Moment" techniques to interrupt or prevent the stress cascade/ response, and a self-talk that created rational thinking to deal with our fears. I realized that harnessing these tools would empower my patients and me to think differently about stress and in the process make us physically, emotionally, and mentally healthier. They would increase our resilience and reserve to weather the unpredictable stressors that knock us for a loop and force us to summon our inner strength so they don't inflict unnecessary harm.

In my current practice, I have identified four categories that I see as vital for building resilience in the face of stress: eat a healthy **D**iet, **M**editate, **W**alk (or engage in some form of exercise), and **S**leep: DMWS™, which you can remember with the mnemonic Don't Mess With Stress™. I even trademarked it! Improving behavior with regard to these four elements comprise what I call the **Don't Mess With Stress™ foundation** for optimal health and resilience. These core lifestyle behaviors provide the framework for you to withstand life's stressors and result in improved psychological, mental, and physical stability and reserve. They allow you to keep calm and make good decisions despite the stress.

This book has been many years in the making, and I am excited to finally be sharing my experience and knowledge with readers like you. Together, day by day, we will learn to manage our stress and achieve greater health and well-being.

Much of what I discuss in this book you may already know. It's how the information is organized, in distinct sections—each with current research and instructions on how to personalize it—that makes it unique.

MY PATH AS A HUMAN BEING

Have you heard the adage, "We teach what we need to learn"? Well, for most of my life, beginning around age five, I have suffered from the effects of stress and anxiety. One of the themes in this book is a lesson I had to learn for myself—the need to give up perfectionism and stop being so rigid and hard on myself. That includes those times when I struggle to manage my own stress or master a technique.

As my dear sister-in-law Tracy so perfectly expresses it: "Even though we can never achieve no stress, we can feel good about the things we CAN do and not punish ourselves for setbacks." It has taken me a long time to stop punishing myself. I still have days when I am not compassionate, accepting, or forgiving of my own failings. I am learning that life is a journey where I will make mistakes and grow from them.

A confession: writing this book was stressful for me. I have always been too worried about others' feelings, wondering what they think of me, trying to please and afraid to displease. I have had trouble with procrastination and time management. Negative self-talk and perfectionism round out the list of my personal obstacles. All these qualities contribute to my stress, on top of the stressors flooding in from external input.

You might ask, why can't a stress "expert" who is writing a book on the subject manage her own stress? Because I am human and haven't completely mastered my wants, needs, and urges in the moment. But I have come a long way, and that's why I believe you can too. It also makes me much more compassionate and tolerant of others who have their own demons such as difficulty losing weight or alcoholism.

My own tools and techniques have been invaluable to me in overcoming my personal obstacles. I have made great strides in several areas of the DMWS program, but sometimes I fall off the wagon. When that happens, I try to note how I feel, mind and body, so that next time, perhaps, I will be stronger and more committed.

Recently, I heard the story of a crew team practicing for an important race. Finally, one of the team members asked, "What will move the boat forward?" So, I ask the same of you: will eating a pint of ice cream help me or you deal with stress and power our boat through the water? What we need is a decision to commit to moving that boat forward and courage when the going gets rough.

Writing this book, I pictured the busy woman in her thirties, forties, fifties, or sixties who is struggling to "do it all" in her personal and/or professional life with grace and ease. Why do I specify women? It is unfortunate, but in

Western culture, women are the likeliest to acknowledge their own mental and physical pain and ask for help. In men, such admissions can be seen as weakness.

Perhaps this is part of the reason women live longer. Whether a full-time mom, a single working woman, a mother who has a demanding career, or a caretaker for elderly or disabled parents, we all share the daily stressors of surviving in this world. Don't get me wrong: men will benefit from the book just as much, if they acknowledge their stress and are open to new practices.

BORN TO BE STRESSED

Let's revisit, briefly, my own journey in pursuit of inner calm. I have struggled with anxiety and stress most of my life. Even though I consider myself an expert on the subject of stress and speak before large audiences about it, I still have difficulty at times dealing with my stressors. I have to continually recommit to the daily habits, rituals, and practices that create the backbone of my health and well-being. Because stress management has been a lifelong odyssey, I feel that I can bring my personal and professional knowledge and experience in this area to help you, the reader, and ultimately the world.

The term biochemical individuality, coined by the eminent biochemist Roger Williams, PhD in 1956, means that there is great variation among people in anatomy, physiology, brain chemistry, and genetic predispositions and their reactions to the environment. An event that elicits a super-stressed-out reaction in one person might barely faze another. We are all "wired" differently. In my case, there is a family history of anxiety on the maternal side. It can probably be traced to epigenetic changes due to emotional traumas in previous generations that have been passed down and expressed. A 2018 study titled "Intergenerational transmission of paternal trauma among US Civil War ex-POWs"[1] supports this theory. Other findings in the rapidly advancing field of epigenetics suggest, conversely, that a healthy lifestyle can mitigate, modulate, and perhaps prevent the expression of "bad" genes.

I recall clearly the first time I felt the stress response. I was in fifth grade and had to make a presentation in front of the class. I still remember the dryness of my mouth and my pounding heart as I awaited my turn.

In junior high, my father was the principal of my school. There probably was pressure on me to excel, although I think it was mainly internally generated. I had an almost obsessive drive to be the best or achieve the most. I suspect I was trying to gain approval and recognition from my parents and others.

During eighth grade, I went into a deep depression triggered by taunting from a classmate, lack of acceptance by my other peers, and possibly jealousy because my father was principal of my school. My body began to change, and I started to have trouble speaking in class—an occasional stutter or problems getting words out. My parents never took me for psychotherapy or counseling. I did speak with a guidance counselor, who just told me, "I know how you feel." After several months, my mother finally called the mother of the kid who had been emotionally and socially torturing me. Life improved after that. I wish I had let her do that earlier.

In high school, I struggled with wanting to be in the popular cliques, even though I didn't necessarily have much in common with the girls in them. I remember once sitting down with a group of sort-of-popular girls in the lunchroom, and one of them saying, "What is she doing here?" She pointed to me, filling me with shame and embarrassment.

Many young women suffer from feelings of inferiority. Without help, these issues can persist throughout our lives, holding us back interpersonally and professionally. To some extent, that was true of me. At this point in my life, I am starting to feel worthy much of the time.

A TURNING POINT

In high school, I learned Transcendental Meditation. Even at 17, I was aware of the concept of stress—as well as feeling it in myself. I started to do TM but was not committed to it and took a break while I was at Princeton University. I certainly could have used it then. I don't think I grasped the benefits of meditation at that time.

At Princeton, I was surrounded by people who had been at the top of their high school classes. Over time I made close friends there and ended up having a positive experience, though it was peppered with doubts raised by my somewhat low self-esteem.

Ironically, while getting a master's degree in physiology at Georgetown University, I wrote my thesis on the physiology of TM, even though I had not practiced TM for some time. Clearly my subconscious was trying to tell me something. As a teaching fellow for two courses, I definitely felt the effects of stress. I experienced involuntary fluttering of my eyelids—the scientific term is fasciculation.

Medical school, for me, was a stressful yet powerful experience. I chose a residency in Family Medicine, as it was the most mind-body of the specialties. A chance encounter that I will relate in the Meditation chapter led me back to TM after a 13-year hiatus.

I have also since tried other meditation techniques, including Art of Living and Mindfulness Meditation. I find that Mindfulness Mediation, done consistently, can affect how I respond in tense situations. I have not been regular with the practice, as I use TM as the base.

IS STRESS INEVITABLE?

Stress is determined by our perception of a situation. If we believe an event or situation is stressful, we will react accordingly.

As described above, the conditions of my life during my first years in the group medical practice were inherently stressful. Meditation helped, but it didn't change the stressful conditions of my working life or my ability to cope with them. During that period, I suffered at various times from anxiety, depression, hair loss, and skin conditions.

One day I saw an elderly female patient who was wheelchair-bound and lived alone. I had the thought: *probably no one touches her*. I remember putting my hand on her shoulder and thinking that what she really needed was TLC—tender loving care. Experiences such as this one pushed me to think that there had to be a more holistic way to practice medicine. After an ultimatum from administrators that I see 25 patients per day, I left my job and took a year off to contemplate and educate myself. This breather led to my decision to open my own office practicing Integrative Medicine. Since that time, I have taken many courses in Integrative Medicine and have become certified in Functional Medicine, which is a framework for evaluating patients in a "deeper dive." Instead of hurrying patients out, I keep asking, "Anything else on your mind?" and holding a long pause until I'm sure there *are* no other concerns.

I finally have the time to attempt to get to the root of my patients' issues.

WALKING ON COALS

Several years later, I took several courses with the self-improvement guru Tony Robbins. I walked on hot coals, barely getting singed. Tony primed us with neurolinguistic techniques to get through the potentially risky experience of walking on the coals. He told us to look up and keep repeating the phrase, "cool moss, cool moss, cool moss." That experience was more than 14 years ago, and to this day, I still remember the feeling of "cool moss" under my feet. Wow!!! This kind of experience and training made me wonder about the true power of our minds over our bodies.

THE TRIUMPH OF THE HUMAN SPIRIT

My journey of self-discovery and gaining personal mastery continues, and I am closer than ever to a life filled with optimal health, joy, abundance, and fulfillment. Like most of you, I have faced the loss of love ones, devastating relationship breakups, and daunting career challenges. But the human spirit is tough to break, and I am still here and thriving. My life experiences and thirst for knowledge and betterment have allowed me to bring you this book. May it help you master your stress, and in the process create a healthier, resilient, and more powerful you!

The ultimate bonus of successful stress management: if all of us were to practice the Don't Mess With Stress™ tools in this book, we would be healthier and happier, and as a result, our wisdom, kindness, and understanding would make the world a better place. Now let's find out how.

Endnote

1 Costa, Dora & Yetter, Noelle & DeSomer, Heather. (2018). Intergenerational transmission of paternal trauma among US Civil War ex-POWs. Proceedings of the National Academy of Sciences. 115. 201803630. 10.1073/pnas.1803630115.

CHAPTER 1
DIET, STRESS, AND YOU

"Tell me what you eat and I will tell you what you are."

Anatehlem-Brillat-Savarin (1755-1826)

BUILDING RESILIENCE

"WE ARE WHAT WE EAT" is the more familiar version of the famous quote by Anatehlem-Brillat-Savarin, the French lawyer and gastronome. What you "take in"—be that food, air, music, words, scenes from the world around you—along with what people you interact with, will, for better or for worse, affect your mind and body.

This chapter focuses on diet and stress. Managing stress requires a foundation to build resilience, allowing us to triumph over our stressors while doing the least amount of damage to our minds and bodies. All four of the DMWS foundational steps are key to reducing stress. However, for some folks, diet is the most important. A nutritious and balanced diet, along with the other three components of the DMWS program, will provide you with the energy, stamina, and vitality to buffer stress and live your life to the fullest.

The goal is to feed your body and mind food that will make them function optimally. This is key to combating stress. Think of a car: if you fill up your car with the wrong fuel, it will not run well. Think of your pet: what is the first question the vet asks when your dog is sick? What did you feed it or what did it eat? In traditional medicine, doctors rarely ask that question.

Eating a diet high in sugar, white flour, alcohol, caffeine, and unhealthy fats can have a profoundly negative impact on your mental and emotional state, let alone your body. A **high glycemic diet**—one that is high in sugar and simple carbohydrates such as refined grains—can raise blood sugar (glucose) levels. It also can make you feel jittery and anxious. Too much caffeine can do the same. A high glycemic diet can also inflame the brain and the body, causing symptoms of anxiety and stress, memory loss, heart disease, and hardening of the arteries.

An unhealthful diet exacerbated by a demanding job or chaotic personal life will absolutely create stress and motivate you to choose even poorer nutritional choices such as junk food. Bottom line: you will be weakening your resilience to stress.

Conversely, imagine that your diet is nutritious and you are getting plenty of sleep. The result will be a healthier gut that enables you to be more resilient to life's stressors.

In this chapter, I identify which foods exacerbate stress and which foods and other natural substances can make you feel calmer and more grounded. I also provide a framework for healthy eating hygiene so you can better digest, absorb, and metabolize your food. Lastly, I recommend supplements that can help decrease stress.

Most of us already know what healthier eating entails, but there are impediments to obtaining the best ingredients, among them access, cost, and the lack of culinary skills to prepare them in a tasty, healthful way. We are fortunate that today many food companies now make it easier to order healthy foods online.

As the food writer Michael Pollan famously wrote:

"Eat food. Not too much. Mostly plants."

Ideally, it is best to eat whole, organic, nutrient-dense foods—fruits, vegetables, and complex grains, wild fatty fish, wild and pasture-raised meats. "Whole foods" have fiber and nutrients that are not removed during processing. When we talk about "whole foods," we mean foods in their unrefined state: a banana rather than banana pudding.

Foods have what we call a **glycemic index**, which is a measure of how high your blood sugar rises when eating that food. The higher the index, the more insulin your body must make. Another term, **glycemic load**, takes into account the glycemic index and also whether you ingest the whole food rather than juices extracted. To make it simple, a whole apple has a much lower glycemic index than the juice extracted from the apple because you are also getting the fiber. For example, a two-cup serving of watermelon has a high glycemic index but a low glycemic load. The juice becomes like a piece of candy, a simple carbohydrate with a high glycemic load that strains the pancreas to make more insulin. The message is to eat complex carbs like whole grains, fruits, and vegetables that require you to chew them to maintain steady blood sugar levels. Whole foods nourish our minds and bodies, keeping us emotionally grounded and filled with energy to deal with the demands of modern life.

Plant-based diets provide the best whole foods. They have many positive health benefits for the brain and body that I discuss further in this chapter. Plant foods also contain fiber, which helps with bowel elimination. Plant foods supply important nutrients and healthy chemicals to help you think more clearly, gain more energy, and feel better.

When buying fresh fruits and vegetables and meats, always look for the USDA round green Organic Seal. For any food to qualify as organic, it must meet the following criteria:

- Organic crops cannot be grown with synthetic fertilizers, synthetic pesticides, or sewage sludge.
- Organic crops cannot be genetically engineered or irradiated.
- Animals must eat only organically grown feed

and can't be treated with synthetic hormones or antibiotics.

- Animals must have access to the outdoors, and hoofed animals must have access to pasture.
- Animals cannot be cloned.
- Also look for a Non-GMO label which certifies that the food has not been produced with genetically modified ingredients.

THE SKINNY ON PROCESSED FOODS

We should limit or avoid **processed foods** that are prepared or processed with artificial additives and other ingredients to enhance or preserve flavor. Most foods that we see on grocery shelves in cans or packages have been processed. Pick up any packaged foods and carefully read the label. See for yourself the list of chemicals, preservatives and coloring that have been added. Typically, you will also find sodium, non-nutritive sweeteners, and unhealthful fats.

The human body was not designed to assimilate processed foods. Unfortunately, we live in a society where processed foods are easily accessible, tempting, and nearly impossible to avoid. Nutritionists label the **Standard American Diet** with the sardonic acronym, **SAD**, because it's unhealthy. This diet adversely affects the microbiome: the bacteria, viruses, and fungi that reside in the gastrointestinal tract. Bad bacteria flourish in a SAD diet and create a gut imbalance that causes food cravings and lowers metabolism. By limiting their consumption, we can avoid the excess sodium, chemicals, non-nutritive sweeteners, and unhealthful fats that stress our bodies and minds.

Unfortunately, processed foods also trigger inflammation in the brain and throughout the body. Research[1] has shown that processed foods raise the level of high-sensitivity C-reactive protein, a marker of inflammation.

Eating processed foods containing sugar increases **Advanced Glycation End Products** or **AGEs**. AGEs result from the binding of sugar (glucose) to fats and proteins. Ironically, AGEs age us, inflame us, and stress our bodies. They can cause memory loss, heart disease, diabetes, and even prematurely age the skin.[2] According to an October 2018 study[3] AGEs can build up in bones, joints, and muscles contributing to chronic diseases that target those areas.

How can we go about reducing these AGE problems? You guessed it! By avoiding processed foods and eating a healthy diet most of the time. Three major U.S. health organizations—the American Heart Association, the American Institute for Cancer Research, and the American Diabetes Association recommend "increasing the consumption of fish, legumes, low-fat milk products, vegetables, fruits, and whole grains and by reducing intake of solid fats, fatty meats, full-fat dairy products, and highly processed foods" to reduce the AGEs created by your diet.[4]

It is also important to note that the way you cook your food can either increase or decrease production of the AGE compounds. Choose poaching, steaming, and stewing over frying, broiling, grilling, or roasting. If you use an acidic marinade such as lemon juice or vinegar before cooking, you can reduce the amount of AGEs produced.

Another reason to reduce your consumption of processed foods such as breads, cakes, cookies, pizza, bagels, muffins, pasta, candy, juices, and sodas is that they are quickly broken down into the simplest sugar, glucose, and have a high Glycemic Index as described above. The glucose stresses the pancreas to shoot out insulin. About half an hour after eating a cookie or candy, your body senses low blood sugar. This is called hypoglycemia. The sudden drop in sugar makes you jittery, cranky, irritable, and anxious. Eating whole foods with lots of fiber slows down the release of insulin, making you feel calmer and more grounded.

THE OPTIMAL STRESS-REDUCING DIET

Harvard University recently published a Diet Review of all the major diets. It is available online and worth checking out. There is no one diet for everyone. As Roger Williams says in his book, *Biochemical Individuality*, we are all different and process things in different ways. Even broccoli can be one man's poison and another man's medicine.

When choosing the best diet for you, take into consideration your food preferences as well as any personal health issues. You will need to experiment. The list of diets is seemingly endless: foundational, vegetarian, pescatarian, low lectin, omnivorian, carnivorian, raw, cooked, gluten free, paleo, vegan, ketogenic, Mediterranean, and Flexitarian.

As the Diet Review states upfront, any diet that works for you must be balanced nutritionally, taste good to you and fit in to the demands of your life. Whatever variations in your routine the diet you choose might entail, in the end it must work for your lifestyle. The key is to make things simple. And do not expect to eat perfectly all the time. Take it from Michael Pollan, a professor of science and environmental journalism at the Berkeley Graduate School of Journalism at the University of California, also the author of The Omnivore's Dilemma. Rule 64 in his book, Food Rules, states: "Break the rules once in a while."

What do all healthy diets have in common? Reducing caffeine and sugar. That includes fruit juices, sodas, and sports drinks.[5] Limit alcohol and processed foods. Your staples: whole, organic, wild, pasture-raised foods. Cook your own food if possible and read labels. Many foods, including store-bought tomato sauce, have high levels of added sugar or sugar substitutes like high fructose corn syrup.

Only you can ultimately decide which diet nourishes your body and soul, a diet you can stay with over the years. That may involve more than one false start. Don't give up!

NUTRIENT-DENSE FOODS

Your goal should be to choose food with the greatest nutritional value and the lowest calorie count. Nutrient-dense foods give you the highest quality protein, complex carbohydrates, and healthy fats. Nutrient-deficient diets cause inflammation in the body and contribute to a number of chronic health conditions such as high blood pressure, high cholesterol, diabetes, heart and vascular disease as well as various types of cancer, eating disorders, obesity and tooth decay.

For the highest nutritional value and the lowest calories, consider a **Flexitarian** or **Mediterranean diet**. The Flexitarian meal plan is predominantly plant-based, with the addition of fish, poultry, dairy, and eggs. Very little red meat. The Mediterranean diet emphasizes vegetables, fruits, nuts, beans, whole grains, and olive oil supplemented with fish and limited amounts of poultry and eggs. It rarely includes red meat. Both types of diets have been shown to be anti-inflammatory and health fortifying. The Mediterranean diet has been associated with reduced risk of major chronic diseases including cancer, Parkinson's, Alzheimer's, Type 2 diabetes, and heart disease. An aging brain, in particular, can benefit from such a diet with the reward of sharper memory and increased alertness.

Ann Caldwell and Maureen Shackelford, nutritionists and registered dietitians at Anne Arundel Medical Center in Maryland, are an excellent resource if you're looking for specific ways you can plan your diet to best improve brain function. The following expands on their recommendations:

- **Vegetables**. Cruciferous vegetables include broccoli, cabbage, brussels sprouts, and leafy greens such as kale, chard, and collards. The more color the better. Steaming is an excellent option. The closer they are to raw, the healthier they will be. However, raw vegetables can be hard to digest in any quantity, so they are not an option for those with delicate stomachs.

  "Supertasters" find many foods with strong flavors unpalatable. However, you can learn to like them. If you are one who simply cannot deal with kale, concentrate on the vegetables you like. The fresher they are, the more flavorful they will be. Spices, garlic, and herbs help to make some vegetables more palatable. Try to vary your vegetable intake by "eating the rainbow."

Purple beets today, orange carrots tomorrow, white cauliflower the next day. Different colored vegetables offer different nutrients.

- **Nuts**. All nuts are good for you, but some not as much. Think raw, organic nuts, not cocktail nuts with oodles of salt. Raw almonds and walnuts are particularly good for reducing inflammation. Pistachios have the highest fiber and potassium content. Cashews are an excellent way to add iron and zinc to your diet. If you are pregnant, eat hazelnuts for their high folate content. Macadamia nuts and pecans have the highest calorie counts, but they are also high in mono-unsaturated fat, which can reduce bad LDL cholesterol. Brazil nuts are rich in selenium.

- **Berries**. Seek out the darkest ones—blackberries, blueberries, and cherries—but also strawberries and raspberries. All have been shown to improve brain health and memory. It is best to buy organic berries, if feasible, because conventional berries have a high pesticide concentration.

- **Omega-3 fatty acids**. There are three types of omega 3 fatty acids. Alpha linolenic (ALA) are found in nuts, seeds, and leafy greens. Eicosapentanoic Acid (EPA) and Docosahexanonic Acid (DHA) are found mostly in fatty fish. Research suggests that replenishing omega-3 fatty acids calmed the anxiety of medical students facing exams and patients recovering from heart attacks.[6] It is worth noting that taking more than you need may result in stomach ache, loose stools, and nausea, and even internal bleeding. The memories of young adults as well as aging persons can benefit from a diet rich in fatty acids and DHA. EPA and DHA are essential for brain development during pregnancy and early childhood. They have also been linked to improved heart health, better vision, treatment for Alzheimer's Disease, and reduced inflammatory response.

EPA and DHA are called essential fatty acids because they are produced in small quantities in the body and therefore must be added to our diet through dietary sources such as cold-water fatty fish, including salmon, tuna, sardines, and herring. I would limit the frequency of eating tuna because of high mercury levels or eat canned light tuna, which has been shown to have lower mercury levels than albacore. Essential fatty acids are also found in grass-fed meat, or omega-3 enriched or pasture-raised eggs.

Don't eat fried fish. Opt instead for grilling, baking, or broiling. Don't like fish? You can get omega 3 fatty acids from plant-based foods such as flaxseeds, chia seeds, walnuts, and algae.

- **Don't expect instant results**. You're in this for the long haul! The more consistently you substitute the foods mentioned above for unhealthier options, the more your entire body will glow with good health, inside and out. My personal and clinical experience has led me to conclude that fish oil helps elevate mood and lower stress.

ACTION STEPS

- If you cannot buy fresh fish, buy your fish flash frozen at sea and thaw just before eating.
- Fresh berries not available? Try frozen or dried berries in your steel-cut oatmeal. Consider drying the fruit yourself.

WATER

Our bodies are 60% water, so clearly getting enough water should be a priority. Dehydration leaves us exhausted and in its severe form can kill us quickly. Without enough water, we cannot rid our bodies of waste, regulate our body temperature, or keep our joints lubricated.

How much water do we actually need? We've been told to drink 8 glasses a day. You could also use the formula: half your weight in ounces. The National Academies of Science, Engineering, and Medicine (NASEM) offers a recommendation[7] for much more, but that seems on the high side to me. Thirst tells most of us when to drink, though we are all not equally attuned to our body's needs. We get about 20% of our required liquid intake from food. If you have been exercising or outside in extreme heat you will need more fluids. If you have a urinary tract infection, the flu, or are pregnant you will need more fluids as well.

You are probably drinking enough fluids if your urine is colorless or light yellow. If you are feeling hungry, try a glass of water first. Hunger is easily mistaken for thirst.

It is possible to drink too much water, but that is not a concern for most of us.

Buy a filtering system even if it is just a special pitcher with a filter you keep in your refrigerator so that your water is as pure and tasty as possible. If you cut soft drinks out of your diet, you may come to realize there is nothing more delicious and thirst-quenching than good old H_2O. Ideally, room-temperature filtered water is best.

ACTION STEP
- Buy a high quality, leak-proof water bottle, preferably stainless steel or glass, and carry it with you all the time.

SUPPLEMENTS SHOWN TO REDUCE STRESS

Fresh, organically grown, raw, or gently and healthfully cooked vegetables provide the best nutrients. Ideally you should be getting your vitamins and minerals from such foods. However, if nutrient-rich food is not available to you or your lifestyle makes it difficult to shop organic or cook healthfully, taking supplements is a good idea.

You will want to choose supplements by vitamin manufacturers that use the highest quality, freshest ingredients. Ask your physician or health provider for recommendations.

- **Vitamin B Complex**. B-vitamin deficiency can cause moodiness and neurologic issues. Vegans should supplement with Vitamin B12 because the only significant source of Vitamin B12 is from animals. Whatever your diet, consider a B complex multivitamin. MDLinx, a website whose well researched articles are geared to physicians and healthcare professionals who face constant daily stress, recommends five supplements in particular. The first of these is B vitamins. One study[8] found that 90 days of taking a high dose of multivitamin B complex significantly reduced confusion, depression, fatigue, and anxiety. Once again, consult your physician about the dose best for you. Excessive amounts (of anything) are bad for you.

- **Vitamin C (L-ascorbic acid)**. With regard to stress, there is evidence for Vitamin C strengthening immune function, and it has a role in regulating cortisol production from the adrenal glands. Eating at least 5 servings of fruits and vegetables per day should provide the recommended daily amounts of

Vitamin C. However, you might need more when you are sick or to prevent infection. In its role as an important antioxidant, Vitamin C can benefit you in many other ways, including gum health.[9] Buffered Vitamin C might be easier on your stomach. Recommended doses vary and smokers need at least 125 mg per day. Because Vitamin C can contribute to kidney stones, please speak with your physician before taking supplemental Vitamin C if you have a history of kidney stones or if you might be at risk.

- **Vitamin D**. Interest in Vitamin D has picked up recently due to the COVID-19 pandemic. Studies indicate that many patients with severe complications of all kinds are deficient in Vitamin D.[10] Vitamin D deficiency has been linked to many medical conditions including anxiety, memory loss, bone disorders, cardiovascular diseases, diabetes, autoimmune diseases, and cancer. An adequate supply in your body can enhance immunity. As we get older, we do not absorb this vitamin as well. In addition, those who live in cloudy climates, stay indoors, or are overweight may well benefit from a supplement.

  The main food sources of Vitamin D are fatty fish, animal liver, fish oils, and egg yolks, so if your diet excludes those items, you should consider a supplement. However, you do not want to overdose on Vitamin D, as dangerous levels can build up gradually and damage the kidneys. A safe dose had been thought to be 1000–4000 IU (25–100 micrograms), but more recent research[11] calls into question past studies and that recommendation. If you are concerned about your levels of Vitamin D, request a serum, 25-hydroxy vitamin D blood test from your healthcare professional and let him or her help determine the optimum dose for you. The actual number of people with genuine Vitamin D deficiency is believed to be low, something like 6%.[12] Most people get enough from 5-30 minutes of exposure to sunlight. Does Vitamin D help combat stress? More research is needed. However, a deficiency will definitely add to it.

- **Zinc and magnesium**. Zinc and magnesium are both minerals essential to our health and well-being. A November 2017 study[13] outlines the reasons these minerals are particularly essential to patients suffering from depression. What are the causes of poor zinc and magnesium absorption from food requiring a need for supplements? 1) Consuming unusual amounts of vegetables (vegetarians), 2) taking calcium supplements (postmenopausal women), and 3) being pregnant (the fetus depletes your mineral levels). Chronic stress and emotional pain also increase the need for supplements of these minerals. Referring to the study above[14], boosting levels of zinc and magnesium was found to decrease anxiety in stressed rats as well as anger and depression in humans. Too much zinc can be harmful, so get your levels checked before taking a supplement.

- **Omega-3 fish oil supplements**. If you are eating two servings of fatty fish a week, you may not need omega-3 fish oil supplements.

DIET AND YOUR GUT

The gut refers to the entire gastrointestinal tract but more commonly describes the large intestine or colon. In the gut resides the **microbiome**, the complicated and diverse system of microbiota, the community of bacteria, archaea, viruses, yeast, and other fungi. A 2019 study[15] shows that in addition to diet, stress and mood affect your gut microbiome and can cause inflammation in your gut and your body. The reverse is also true—the microbiome and inflammation in the gut can wreak havoc on your diet, stress, and mood. A roiling gastrointestinal system can lead directly to a foul mood. There is a biological reason people with Irritable Bowel Syndrome (IBS) and other bowel issues are more likely to become depressed and anxious.

There is an additional nervous system in the gut called the **Enteric Nervous System**. Enteric refers to the intestines. The Enteric Nervous System is also called our second brain. It contains 100 million nerve cells lining the esophagus to the stomach, the intestines, and the rectum. Perhaps that is the origin of the term "gut feeling" when describing a feeling that cannot be explained logically.

Many neurotransmitters that are made in the brain are also made in the GI tract. In fact, 90% of the body's serotonin, as an article in *Medical News Today*[16] states, the hormone associated with "regulat(ing) mood and social behavior, appetite and digestion, sleep, memory, and sexual desire and function, is made in the gut."

The microbiome has been shown to cause stress and anxiety and influence mood. A 2017 study[17] indicated that probiotics given to Japanese medical students were shown to help the students sleep better and reduce stress.

High glycemic junk food can affect the gastrointestinal tract. A healthy diet results in a healthy microbiome, which in turn produces healthy neurotransmitters just like those made in the brain that improve your mood and lower your stress.

A March 2020 study[18] showed that an unhealthy microbiome can cause depression. Just one course of antibiotics can wipe out a lot of a person's gut microbiome and can increase anxiety and depression.

PREBIOTICS, PROBIOTICS, AND YOUR GUT

Recent research indicates that certain foods and

supplements called prebiotics and probiotics can improve gut health, help decrease inflammation, and improve our immune system. Ideally, you should get prebiotics and probiotics through food. Prebiotics come from plant-based carbohydrates such as fruits, vegetables, cereals, and grains. They are the food for the intestinal bacteria, including garlic, onions, oats, and barley. Probiotics are healthy bacteria and yeasts that can crowd out the "bad" bacteria and yeast and restore a more normal microbial balance in the gut. There is an exciting emerging field that is studying "psychobiotics"—probiotics that influence the brain, mood, stress, and neurodegenerative conditions such as Alzheimer's disease, Parkinson's disease, and autism spectrum disorder.

Fermented foods are the best source of probiotics:

- **Yogurt**. Choose one with active or live cultures and no sugar.
- **Kefir**, which is usually safe for people with lactose intolerance.
- **Fermented cabbage**, such as unpasteurized sauerkraut and kimchi; their efficacy will depend on the raw ingredients and the fermentation process.
- **Fermented soybeans**, found in tempeh patties, miso soup—which also includes a type of fungus called koji—and natto, a Japanese breakfast staple mixed with rice; its high quantities of Vitamin K2 are said to increase bone density.

- **Kombucha**, a green or black tea drink fermented with bacteria and yeast
- **Fermented cucumbers**, i.e., pickles, but only those cured in salt and water.
- **Traditional buttermilk**—not the cultured kind.

Probiotic Supplements: The jury is out on how much and what types of "good" bacteria are best to take. Not every brand can be trusted, so be sure to speak with your healthcare professional before taking any supplements or probiotics, especially if you have a severe medical condition or just had surgery.

I recommend that patients take a probiotic called Saccharomyces Boulardi when they are taking antibiotics. This is a special type of yeast that might prevent a severe antibiotic-associated diarrhea called Clostridioides difficile (C. diff). Antibiotics can also cause vaginal yeast infections.

Food sensitivities, lactose intolerance, and allergies could potentially be improved by probiotics.

ALCOHOL AND STRESS

Unfortunately, when people are stressed, they may resort to unhealthy behaviors such as drinking excessive alcohol. Alcohol might temporarily calm you down, but in the long run it has been found to increase anxiety.

Chronic drinking can lead to depletion of B vitamins, especially B12, which can lead to psychological issues.

Alcohol can do a number on the digestive system, causing gastritis, ulcers, and GERD. Alcohol destroys brain cells and damages the liver and has been associated with breast cancer.

Alcohol should be considered empty calories and can lead to weight gain.

Wait! Isn't one glass of wine good for you? For a long time, conventional wisdom told us that **polyphenols** in red wine help protect the heart. But the jury's out, based on the weak evidence supporting this claim. What about **resveratrol**, which not only protects the heart but is anti-aging? Perhaps, though red wine contains only miniscule amounts of resveratrol and requires excessive consumption to gain any benefit. Limited alcohol is allowed in the Mediterranean diet.

The current recommendation is don't start drinking alcohol to improve your health. People who choose to drink should limit themselves to one serving of alcohol per day for women, and up to 2 servings per day for men.

Here is the way Harvard Health Publishing defines one beverage of alcohol:

- 12 ounces of regular beer
- 5 ounces of wine
- 1.5 ounces of 80-proof distilled spirits
- 1 ounce of 100-proof spirits.

For some people, just cutting their alcohol intake to one drink or going completely without is enough to make them lose their extra pounds. Just don't indulge the sugar craving that may take its place.

ACTION STEPS

- Mitigate cravings for alcohol or sugary sodas by substituting a healthier liquid "treat": decaffeinated coffee, herbal tea, or fizzy water (consider buying a SodaStream) with a small amount of juice.
- Give yourself a break from alcohol, even if just for a few days or a week.

If you believe you have a real problem, seek professional help or join Alcoholics Anonymous (AA).

CREATE A HEALTHFUL KITCHEN ENVIRONMENT

Stress can make you overeat because you crave junk food in the form of sweet or salty snacks.

One of the ways to control overeating and eating less healthy foods is to **exert environmental control**. This means that you should not keep sugary snacks, ice cream, potato chips, M&Ms, and other goodies in your kitchen cabinets to tempt you when stress gets you down. One of my physician colleagues once said that he asked his wife not to bake chocolate chip cookies when he is home because he will eat them. He knows what triggers unhealthy choices for him.

Stock your kitchen with healthful snacks such as apples, grapes, nuts, celery, and carrots, so you can reach for them easily. People who struggle with portion control may not want to keep nuts around, unless packaged in small amounts.

EATING HYGIENE

I think by now we are all washing our hands as frequently as possible, especially before handling food and eating. What other habits can we cultivate to promote more conscious consumption and better digestion?

- **Make eating its own conscious activity**. Don't eat when you are working at your computer or reading. I have to confess that I sometimes do this. But I am realizing that I am not getting the full pleasure out of eating my meal, and the unpleasant news that I am reading while eating is not good for my digestion.
- **Concentrate on what you are eating**. Look at each food on your plate and anticipate its taste, texture, and odor.
- **Chew**. This may seem obvious, but how many of us gulp down our food as quickly as possible? Chewing enables us to taste and savor each bite. The more we break our food down before it enters the digestive tract, the easier it will be to digest it.

Digestion begins in the mouth with our saliva that contains digestive enzymes. Let it do its part and avoid overburdening the gut. Food that isn't broken down by saliva may cause bacterial overgrowth, resulting in passing gas, burping, constipation, and leaky gut syndrome.

- **Take your time**. If you don't take your time while you eat, how will your brain get the message that you are full? The best way to control weight is to ask yourself with every bite if you have had enough.

- **Dine with people you like**. You'll enjoy your food more. Eating with people you don't like will upset you and your digestion.

- **Don't eat when you're upset**. Negative emotions interfere with digestion. It is better to wait before eating if you are upset.

- **Cook it yourself**. Restaurant food tastes great but it can be packed with calories, unhealthy additives, too much salt, and the wrong kind of fats. Even if you've never cooked, there have never been so many free online resources to get you started. You will feel empowered with your new culinary skills and have fun, too. You will gain understanding of the value of various foods and the variety of healthful cooking techniques.

- **Do not use the term "diet"** in conjunction with weight loss. Eat and drink with your health in mind and your body may find its "normal" weight.

ACTION STEPS

- Try the **Mindful Eating Exercise**[19] recommended by Linda Smith at Duke Integrative Medicine. In short, savor the complete sensual experience of consuming something you find delicious; e.g., one raisin, grape or a piece of dark chocolate.

- Try an experiment with chewing each forkful of food 30 times. Close your eyes and taste the difference. You will probably eat less food as well.

THE BUZZ ABOUT CAFFEINE

For most people, coffee is healthy if consumed in moderation. Like black and green tea, it has anti-inflammatory properties and is an antioxidant, helping cells stay healthy by combatting free radicals—unstable molecules caused by such factors as cigarettes, alcohol, ultraviolet light, and yes, stress, which can lead to cancer and other chronic diseases.

The best outcome for coffee drinkers is increased alertness, energy, and concentration. But overdo it, and you can become jittery and irritable, even develop heart palpitations. The definition of "overdo" varies widely between individuals. For people with caffeine sensitivity, a little goes a long way and even one cup can interfere with sleep.

Coffee might contribute to Gastroesophageal Reflux (GERD). Most of us will want to avoid drinking more than one or two cups per day.

Once again, pay attention to how you feel. It's up to you to decide what amount of coffee, if any, benefits your body. Ask yourself if it increases your anxiety and stress. And watch the flavorings. If you're loading up your coffee with cream, sugar, and hazelnut syrup, you're packing it with calories and unhealthful substances and undoing any health benefits. A grande Starbucks Caffè Mocha with 2% milk and whipped cream contains 360 calories, 14 grams of fat, and 35 grams of sugar.[20]

ACTION STEPS
- Cut down on caffeine gradually by substituting decaf or mixing regular and decaf.
- Opt for green or white tea, which contain less caffeine than black.

GENETICALLY MODIFIED ORGANISMS (GMO)

Here is yet another reason to avoid processed foods: quite a few contain genetically modified ingredients, and companies do not need to divulge this fact. The FDA does not require any safety testing or research that show these foods are safe. What does this mean for us? The processed food we eat may contain genes, bacteria, and viruses that make them toxic to some consumers. Someone who is not normally allergic to a particular product may be allergic to the GMO version. These products may also be 1) less nutritious, 2) suppress immunity, 3) contribute to antibiotic resistance, and 4) cause cancer.

Non-Nutritive Sweeteners

While we're on the subject of coffee and tea, let's take a hard look at non-nutritive sweeteners (NNS). Aspartame, neotame, saccharin, sucralose, and stevia. The FDA says they're safe, but are they? Research[21] suggests that they induce dysbiosis (imbalance of the microbiome) and also increase pre-diabetes, which may lead to type-2 diabetes in previously healthy people. Also, when you drink a diet soda, your body isn't fooled. That diet soda makes it crave the real thing. The body wants the calories it has been deprived of but promised, and it will seek to obtain them through some other means. That means NNS use is more likely to make you *gain* weight.

All the NNS we consume show up later in groundwater and tap water, and one 2018 study implied they caused heart defects in newborns.[22]

What about agave nectar? Sorry, no, although it is a better option than refined sugar. It has a lower GI (glucose index) initially, but long-term use may increase your chances of developing fatty liver disease and high cholesterol and lead to type-2 diabetes.

Stevia, made from a plant, is considered a more

"natural" sweetener and also has zero calories. It may even have some health benefits. I would still recommend limiting non-nutritive sweeteners in general.

ACTION STEP

- Do a food experiment—go off sugar and artificial sweeteners for one week. How do you feel? Does food taste better? Do you feel less tired? Do you have more energy? Is your mind more alert?

HEALTHY COMFORT FOOD

Although the following foods are good for you, it goes without saying that you should consume them in moderation.

- **Dark Chocolate**. Women have long suspected that chocolate helps in times of stress, and now there's science to back them up. Studies have shown that dark chocolate eaters rid themselves of stress hormones by excreting them in their urine. Not only does cocoa relieve stress, but it also helps you think more clearly and cheers you up. But if you want the benefits without the sugar and other additives, choose high quality dark chocolate. Adding a square or two of chocolate daily can greatly reduce chronic anxiety. However, for people sensitive to caffeine, dark chocolate does contain caffeine. They could experience side effects like jitteriness and palpitations.

- **Oatmeal** is the ultimate comfort food. Plus, it fills you up and is easy to digest. We also know now that oatmeal can reduce levels of stress hormones and help you stay calmer by releasing serotonin.
- **Dates** are low glycemic, meaning that they are not as likely to make your blood sugar spike. They are also an excellent source of vitamins, minerals, and fiber.

ACTION STEP

- Next time you make pasta or pizza, try substituting 1) vegetables for meat, 2) hard cheeses for soft ones, and 3) whole grain flour products for those made with all-purpose flour.

FOOD SENSITIVITIES AND THE ELIMINATION DIET

People who crave certain unhealthy foods and/or struggle with excess weight may have undiagnosed food sensitivities, also known as intolerances and allergies. The same food that you can't seem to stop eating may be the cause of your anxiety and fatigue. Foods can also cause brain fog, abdominal bloating, diarrhea, constipation, and rashes, thus lowering your resilience and stressing your immune system.

If these food sensitivities remain unidentified, they can worsen over time, causing digestive issues and allergic reactions, even life-threatening ones. Many of us suspect that a particular food does not work for our bodies, but often the culprit is an ingredient hidden in several products that we eat frequently. This is where the Elimination Diet[23] comes in.

The usual offenders are gluten (most commonly found in bread, pasta, crackers, cakes, and cookies), dairy, corn, soy, eggs, citrus, and tree nuts. Begin your investigation by eliminating all the potential offenders, then reintroduce one of them after about three weeks and see what happens. If you have a reaction, avoid that food for the time being. Then add the next item and so on. Why are you "sensitive" to this ingredient? Perhaps you don't digest it well, and it has become an irritant. Improving digestion might mean that you can reintroduce it at some point. Don't try to do this alone. It is best to consult your physician to get to the bottom of your sensitivity.

THE BEST TIMES TO EAT

There is an old saying: eat breakfast like a king, lunch like a prince, and dinner like a pauper. Eating a nutritious breakfast and lunch is definitely important, and recent research shows that it is better to eat most of your calories during the day and eat a light dinner on the early side. Evidence suggests that those periods of fasting between meals may help you avoid type-2 diabetes and slow down aging.[24]

What about **intermittent fasting**?[25] The most popular version is the 16/8 method, but it could put you into ketosis, which is a fat-burning state that is dangerous for some people. You skip breakfast and only eat during an 8-hour period, fasting for 16 hours between your last meal and your next meal. If you try this, eat your last meal or dinner at least 3 hours before bedtime because it is better for your brain health. Eating earlier decreases the chance of you having GERD at night. Don't try something like this if you have an eating disorder, diabetes, or other medical condition, and always consult a health professional before starting a fasting program or any extreme diet.

Most people would find the more extreme forms of intermittent fasting hard going. But fasting between your early dinner and breakfast? Isn't this when we sleep anyway? Absolutely!

ACTION STEPS
- Try putting your fork down between each bite.
- Assemble everything you intend to eat on your plate in advance.

ONWARD

The purpose of this book is to help you fill your toolbox with healthy habits for when stress begins to oppress. If you're interested in finding more information about the subjects touched upon here, I recommend the following websites:

- Health.Harvard.edu
- Healthline.com
- MDLinx.com
- Sciencedaily.com

Think about the information you have read here and what small changes you can make to get started. Perhaps it's just trying a new recipe for kale, cutting down on your alcohol consumption, and chewing more. You might be inspired to write down your own action plan. Congratulations! You are on your way to a calmer life.

Endnotes

1 Kiecolt-Glaser JK. Stress, food, and inflammation: psychoneuroimmunology and nutrition at the cutting edge. *Psychosom Med*. 2010;72(4):365-369. doi:10.1097/PSY.0b013e3181dbf489.

2 Gkogkolou P, Böhm M. Advanced glycation end products: Key players in skin aging? *Dermatoendocrinol*. 2012;4(3):259-270. doi:10.4161/derm.22028.

3 Chen, J., Lin, X., Bu, C. *et al*. Role of advanced glycation end products in mobility and considerations in possible dietary and nutritional intervention strategies. *Nutr Metab (Lond)* **15,** 72 (2018). https://doi.org/10.1186/s12986-018-0306-7

4 Uribarri J, Woodruff S, Goodman S, et al. Advanced glycation end products in foods and a practical guide to their reduction in the diet. *J Am Diet Assoc*. 2010;110(6):911-16.e12. doi:10.1016/j.jada.2010.03.018.

5 Most sports drinks contain the additive propionate, which has been linked to obesity and diabetes. It is also added to many baked goods to prevent mold and mildew.

6 Kiecolt-Glaser JK, Belury MA, Andridge R, Malarkey WB, Glaser R. Omega-3 supplementation lowers inflammation and anxiety in medical students: a randomized controlled trial. *Brain Behav Immun*. 2011;25(8):1725-1734. doi:10.1016/j.bbi.2011.07.229.

7 The National Academies of Sciences, Engineering, and Medicine recommends about 15.5 cups (3.7 liters) of fluids for men, 11.5 cups (2.7 liters) of fluids a day for women.

8 Stough, Con, Scholey, Andrew, Lloyd, Jenny, Spong, Jo, Myers, Stephen, Downey, Luke A. "The effect of 90-day administration of a high dose vitamin B-complex on work stress." https://doi.org/10.1002/hup.1229. Sept. 8, 2011.

9 Marik PE. "Vitamin C: an essential 'stress hormone' during sepsis." *J Thorac Dis*. 2020;12(Suppl 1):S84-S88. doi:10.21037/jtd.2019.12.64

10 Biesalski HK. Vitamin D deficiency and co-morbidities in COVID-19 patients – A fatal relationship?. *Nfs Journal*. 2020;20:10-21. doi:10.1016/j.nfs.2020.06.001

11 https://nutrition.bmj.com/content/bmjnph/early/2020/05/15/bmjnph-2020-000089.full.pdf

12 Ibid.

13 Dickerman B, Liu J. Do the Micronutrients Zinc and Magnesium Play a Role in Adult Depression?. *Top Clin Nutr*. 2011;26(3):257-267. doi:10.1097/TIN.0b013e3182260d86

14 Ibid.

15 Madison A, Kiecolt-Glaser JK. Stress, depression, diet, and the gut microbiota: human-bacteria interactions at the core of psychoneuroimmunology and nutrition. *Curr Opin Behav Sci*. 2019;28:105-

110. doi:10.1016/j.cobeha.2019.01.011

16   https://www.medicalnewstoday.com/articles/232248

17   https://www.sciencedirect.com/science/article/pii/S1756464617300543

18   Capuco A, Urits I, Hasoon J, et al. Current Perspectives on Gut Microbiome Dysbiosis and Depression. *Adv Ther*. 2020;37(4):1328-1346. doi:10.1007/s12325-020-01272-7

19   https://www.dukeintegrativemedicine.org/dukeimprogramsblog/wp-content/uploads/sites/4/2017/08/Mindful-Eating-Transcript.pdf

20   https://www.insider.com/the-healthiest-and-unhealthiest-drinks-you-can-order-at-starbucks-2018-5

21   Liauchonak I, Qorri B, Dawoud F, Riat Y, Szewczuk MR. Non-Nutritive Sweeteners and Their Implications on the Development of Metabolic Syndrome. Nutrients. 2019;11(3):644. Published 2019 Mar 16. doi:10.3390/nu11030644

22   Archibald AJ, Dolinsky VW, Azad MB. Early-Life Exposure to Non-Nutritive Sweeteners and the Developmental Origins of Childhood Obesity: Global Evidence from Human and Rodent Studies. *Nutrients*. 2018;10(2):194. Published 2018 Feb 10. doi:10.3390/nu10020194

23   Arscott, Sara A., PhD, and Rindfleisch, Adam, MPhil., MD. "The Elimination Diet" pamphlet. https://www.fammed.wisc.edu/files/webfm-uploads/documents/outreach/im/handout_elimination_diet_patient.pdf. UW Integrative Health, School of Medicien and Public Health, University of Wisconsin-Madison.

24   Hana Kahleova, Jan Irene Lloren, Andrew Mashchak, Martin Hill, Gary E Fraser, Meal Frequency and Timing Are Associated with Changes in Body Mass Index in Adventist Health Study 2, The Journal of Nutrition, Volume 147, Issue 9, September 2017, Pages 1722–1728, https://doi.org/10.3945/jn.116.244749

25   Gunnars, Kris, BSc. "Intermittent Fasting 101—The Ultimate Beginner's Guide." https://www.healthline.com/nutrition/intermittent-fasting-guide. Healthline.com. April 20, 2020.

CHAPTER 2

MEDITATION

MEDITATION IS THE NEXT CORNERSTONE in the foundational program, Don't Mess With Stress™.

WHAT CAN MEDITATION DO FOR ME?

Meditation has been around for so long that it's difficult to trace its origins, though the strongest evidence points to India, thousands of years BCE. The major religions of the world all include some form of this ancient practice.

In meditation we seek more than self-knowledge. We aim to go deeper, finding the true core of our beings that escapes us in our busy daily lives. In order to tap into our spirit—however you choose to define that word—we strive through meditation to shut off the noise of daily worries, desires, and responsibilities. Even if you resist the term "spiritual enlightenment," meditation can put life into perspective, help you realize that the parking ticket or even that court appearance is not serious in the general scheme of things. Meditation can help you find moments of calm and joy in the midst of a hectic schedule or during periods of extreme stress.

In modern times, Indian Gurus introduced meditation to the West. One example is Maharishi Mahesh Yogi, who brought Transcendental Meditation to the Western world to promote happiness and world peace. In today's culture, we tend to use meditation to decrease stress, increase self-awareness, and calm the overactive brain.

Meditation is not a substitute for sleep, though both are alternate states of awareness. Various types of meditation alter your consciousness in different ways. In sleep, your body repairs itself, which means levels of stress hormones decrease. Meditation also decreases stress hormones and contributes to mental and physical healing. Your brain waves alter, your breathing deepens, your heart slows. Meditation can in some ways make up for lost sleep, but it can't replace it. It can enhance its healing qualities. And meditation is better than sleep at putting you in the driver's seat of your emotions.

There are many reasons to meditate. Quieting the mind supports better brain and body function. Many studies tout the benefits of meditation, and my own experience and those of my patients and colleagues confirm their results.

THE BENEFITS OF MEDITATION

Here is a list of the major benefits of meditation:

- Decreased stress, measured by the reduced amount of the stress hormone, cortisol.
- A sharper mind, improved memory and cognition[1] (ability to learn and understand).
- Improved feelings of well-being, including happiness and calmness.
- Decreased depression and anxiety.
- Increased physical and mental resilience,[2] resulting in a stronger immune system.[3]
- Decelerated aging[4] due to lengthened telomeres[5] (the caps on the ends of chromosomes).
- Increased energy.
- Decreased pain.[6]
- Better quality sleep, decreased insomnia.
- Lowered blood pressure.[7]
- Decreased inflammation.[8]
- Decreased insulin resistance, making it easier for diabetics to keep their blood sugar levels steady.
- Improved executive function,[9] leading to more reasoned decision making and greater mental efficiency.
- Decreased heart disease.
- Increased creativity.
- Increased productivity.

- Increased healing of psoriasis lesions.[10]
- Improved ability to relax and be aware in the present moment.
- Improved focus.[11]
- Improved emotional intelligence[12]—the ability to empathize with others and therefore get along better with them; also, the ability to keep negative emotions in check.

MY PATH TO MEDITATION

I have always been a "seeker," which led me to investigate meditation when I was only 17 years old. Even then, my stress response was in high gear. My desire to excel in school and be the best that I could be was taking its toll.

I remember seeing a full-page advertisement in the local newspaper for **Transcendental Meditation™**, also known as TM. The tagline was something like "Learn TM to decrease stress" and pointed to a free introductory lecture at one of the local libraries. I signed up to take the course. One of my teachers and a classmate were doing TM as well. I was excited to embark on something so "fringy" and cool.

I thought I was making headway until one of the last sessions of the training when I was scheduled to be picked up by a carpool for tennis lessons. While meditating with others in my TM class at someone's home, I worried about telling my tennis friends what I was doing, fearing it would subject me to ridicule. When my friend rang the bell to collect me for the carpool, I jumped to my feet—not a good thing to do when the body is in a deep state. At that age, I didn't have the coping skills or self-confidence to manage my fearful and insecure thinking and my hypervigilant state.

After I learned how to meditate, I was not consistent with the practice, and I stopped meditating completely when I went to university. I didn't fully appreciate the benefits at that time.

Near the end of my residency training in Family Medicine, a serendipitous experience changed the course of my life. Thirteen years had passed since I'd last meditated. It was the second to last month of my residency, and I had gone on a "home visit" to a patient with my attending physician.

On the way back from the visit, the attending physician stepped on the brakes, exclaiming, "Wait! That's my patient." A woman stood by the road next to her car, which had a bumper sticker reading Transcendental Meditation. The woman had been on her way to the clinic when her car broke down. We gave her a ride to the clinic, and I mentioned that I used to meditate. She told me, "You must meditate twice a day." I said I barely had time to sleep, let alone meditate. She asked me if I remembered how to do it, and once we were back in the clinic, she checked to make sure I was doing the technique correctly. I decided to start meditating twice a day.

Since that incident in 1989, I have meditated regularly, except for a few brief periods. I don't always get my two sessions in, but I am confident that the practice of meditation has helped build my resistance to disease and ability to handle stress and surely affected my brain in other positive ways. In recent years, I have found that meditation relaxes me, centers me, improves my mood, and softens me. It is a balm for my soul and has made a huge difference in my life.

When I don't meditate, I am more irritable and less centered emotionally. After a long, exhausting day, I can meditate and feel rejuvenated and energized. After meditating, I feel calmer and more positive, like a new person in a matter of minutes.

Over the years, I have learned and experimented with other meditative techniques, including the **Art of Living's "Sudarshan Kriya" (SKY)** breathing exercises, **Mindfulness Based Stress Reduction (MBSR)**, and **Qi Gong** (pronounced Chi Gong). I have also taken a few classes in **T'ai Chi** and incorporated yogic practices (yoga) along with TM, SKY, and MBSR.

Several years ago, I went to India and meditated at an Art of Living ashram there. An ashram is a place to meditate, attend yoga classes, rest, and do spiritual practices away from the pressures and responsibilities of everyday life. It was a wonderful experience, especially since I was in the country where meditation reportedly originated.

Recently, I have added back the SKY breathing exercises once a day, usually in the morning before I meditate. Ideally, I do a second meditation before dinner. The SKY breathing is a way to calm the mind and prepare oneself for meditation. On most days I use TM as my base and add SKY breathing and yoga. I intermittently practice Qi Gong and Mindfulness, although I try to be mindful in my daily life. The morning and evening meditations help anchor my day. The evening meditation gives me a second wind, especially when I am more tired than usual.

These meditation techniques help me "go inside" and "be" with myself, so I can learn and evolve. They also help me relax, decrease my stress, and allow me to be more deliberate with my thoughts and actions. I believe they have helped increase my resilience and strengthen my immune system.

Meditation is not a panacea or cure, but it definitely helps to calm down the nervous system so that the body and mind can function optimally.

HOW TO CHOOSE A MEDITATION TECHNIQUE

With so many meditation practices to choose from, it is easy to get overwhelmed. All of these techniques can lead to similar benefits.[13] In addition to TM, Mindfulness,[14] and SKY breathing, there are sitting meditations, lying-down meditations, walking meditations, "mantra"-based meditations, chanting meditations, lovingkindness meditations, breathing meditations, insight meditation (Vipassana), open-focus meditations, Ziva Meditation, and the moving meditations of the ancient Chinese techniques of T'ai Chi and Qi Gong, to name a few. There are also many apps that offer different meditation experiences, including Headspace and Insight Timer, that are also quite helpful.

LET'S GET STARTED

For those of you who wish to go deeper, I want to tell you a little more about three techniques that have solid research behind them—**TM**, **Mindfulness Meditation**, and the **SKY technique**. The **Art of Living** organization also teaches a meditation practice. These all have official websites you can refer to for more information. I recommend starting with one technique. When you are ready to expand your horizons, you may wish to look into the others. They are easy to pick up and taught by certified teachers. Since the pandemic, many of these courses are now offered virtually.

TM and SKY techniques are taught for a few hours a day over a few days. Mindfulness Meditation courses usually last eight weeks. You can learn more at tm.org and artofliving.org. You can also search online for local Mindfulness Based Stress Reduction Courses (MBSR).

Transcendental Meditation is a "mantra"-based meditation. A mantra is a Sanskrit sound your teacher gives you to use in your meditations. As you meditate with TM, you transcend and release stress, and physiologically your mind and body settle down. TM puts you in a state of "restful alertness."

In **Mindfulness Meditation**, you focus (gently) on breathing. Upon realizing that your mind has started to form thoughts, you shift your awareness back to the breath. This puts you squarely in the present moment. Mindfulness can help you deal with unproductive thoughts, moodiness, anxiety, pain, and many other issues. It also can create "space" to give you more options to respond instead of reflexively reacting. This happened to me once. I was in my office, and something happened that might have caused me to react in a negative way. Instead, my reaction took place in something like slow motion. When I went to respond to the situation, there seemed to be a momentary pause that gave me time to choose a more thoughtful response. That was a profound experience.

Any meditation method you choose will help put you into a more peaceful, "parasympathetic" mode. That means your heartrate and respiration will slow down, and you'll become calmer. You will be less apt to overreact to stress, responding more appropriately to the situation at hand. Better yet, any meditation will likely improve your overall health and well-being.

INTRODUCING MEDITATION

For beginners, an easy way to start is with a simple meditation.

I believe in taking baby steps when learning something new. Start by meditating for just a few minutes. You will still benefit.

Ideally, you should meditate in a quiet environment. But you can meditate anywhere—even with noise in the background, though I'd advise against meditating in a place like the subway where it's best to remain alert.

Why don't you try and meditate with me right now? I will walk you through it.

We are going to meditate for 10 minutes. Don't stress about the time unless you have to be somewhere, and if so, then set a timer with a gentle, soothing alarm.

Here we go ....

- Sit comfortably in a chair or on a bed or cushion. If in bed, avoid having your head touching your pillows, as you might fall asleep. You are aiming for a peaceful waking state.
- Close your eyes.
- Let your hands rest easily in your lap or wherever

they feel comfortable.

- Let your shoulders relax.
- Sit quietly for about a half a minute and then, slowly, gently, focus your awareness on your breathing as it moves in and out of your nose. Before you know it, you will probably become aware of having thoughts concerning your future activities or perhaps doubts about the purpose of this meditation. When you realize that you are having thoughts, gently shift your attention back to the breath. Feel the air move through your nostrils. Thoughts will continue to come. Even in mid-thought, gently shift your attention and awareness back to the breath moving in and out through your nose. If you haven't set an alarm, you can open your eyes briefly to check the time. When your 10 minutes is up, continue to sit for a few minutes. Slowly open your eyes. Rub your hands together and move your legs to increase your heart rate and come back into the room.

Do you feel calmer?

You can repeat this meditation during the day as needed to calm and refresh yourself. You may find that a meditation session changes your perspective of some current challenge.

Traditionally, meditating before bed isn't recommended

because it may put you to sleep. However, for people who have insomnia, meditating can help them relax and fall asleep.

The goal of mindfulness, however, isn't to put you sleep but to make you more aware of the present moment, so you'll want to experiment with meditating at other times of day when you can stay awake. Ideally, you would meditate for ten minutes in the morning before breakfast and then again before dinner. After a week, ask yourself if your new routine has clear benefits for you. If so, keep doing it.

If 10 minutes a day is longer than you can manage, know that even one minute of meditation is better than nothing. Slowly increase to 10 minutes once a day, and then to 20 minutes once a day. Ideally, to get the maximum benefits, you will meditate twice a day.

A MEDITATION JOURNAL

Meditation can be a powerful tool for addressing stress in the moment. It gives you literal breathing space in a crisis or just a powerful pause in the midst of a busy day.

Keeping a journal of your meditation sessions is an effective way of acknowledging the benefits but also addressing the inevitable doubts and frustrations that come with making any significant changes in your routine. All feelings are valid, and there is no downside to examining them.

Start by recording your current commitment to your practice.

For instance: "My goal for this week: 10 minutes of mindfulness meditation in the morning when I wake up and 10 minutes in the late afternoon before dinner, or if my schedule doesn't permit that, 10 minutes before bed."

Write down your 3 reasons for meditating, e.g.:

- It will calm me down.
- It will make me more thoughtful and centered.
- It will help me be calmer and more rational in stressful situations.

Now write down your reasons for not meditating, for example:

- I don't want to.
- I don't have the time.
- I don't think it is going to work.

At night, before you go to sleep, reflect on your recent sessions, for example:
- I felt calmer today.
- My attitude was consistently more positive.
- I was able to deal with Mr. X's complaint without losing my cool.
- I slept better last night.

Or ….

- I was in a bad mood this morning, and meditation didn't help.
- I skipped this morning's session because my alarm didn't go off and found that I was much more irritable.

It's good to acknowledge both positive steps forward as well as backsliding. As with any new routine, you will probably not be 100% compliant. If so, forgive yourself and try again.

In this chapter, I have not focused on yoga. **Yoga**, the discipline of postures and breathing and meditation, is a powerful adjunct to the meditations I have discussed. I encourage you, the reader, to take classes in yoga to get the full benefits of this powerful group of practices. It's important that a teacher monitor your progress; otherwise, you may inadvertently perform the poses in a way that can cause injury.

FINAL THOUGHTS

Research shows that the effects of meditation are incremental.[15] In other words, the more you meditate, the more you benefit. Your brain starts to change in good ways. The hippocampus—the memory center of your brain that shrinks with stress and dementia—has been shown to enlarge after consistent meditation practice.[16] Meditation also changes your gray matter by improving your ability to focus. You may find it easier to learn a new skill, retain knowledge, and keep negative emotions in check.

It's important to start small. It bears repeating that even one minute of meditation is beneficial. Observe how you feel in the quiet. Review the benefits of meditation listed in this chapter and connect with how they can enhance your life. Give it a try for a month and see how you feel.

Endnotes

1 Deepak KK. Meditation induces physical relaxation and enhances cognition: A perplexing paradox. Prog Brain Res. 2019;244:85-99. doi: 10.1016/bs.pbr.2018.10.030. Epub 2019 Jan 3. PMID: 30732847.

2 Kwak S, Lee TY, Jung WH, et al. The Immediate and Sustained Positive Effects of Meditation on Resilience Are Mediated by Changes in the Resting Brain. *Front Hum Neurosci.* 2019;13:101. Published 2019 Mar 26. doi:10.3389/fnhum.2019.00101

3 Black DS, Slavich GM. Mindfulness meditation and the immune system: a systematic review of randomized controlled trials. *Ann N Y Acad Sci.* 2016;1373(1):13-24. doi:10.1111/nyas.12998

4 Luders E, Cherbuin N, Kurth F. Forever Young(er): potential age-defying effects of long-term meditation on gray matter atrophy. Front Psychol. 2015 Jan 21;5:1551. doi: 10.3389/fpsyg.2014.01551. PMID: 25653628; PMCID: PMC4300906.

5 Conklin QA, Crosswell AD, Saron CD, Epel ES. Meditation, stress processes, and telomere biology. *Curr Opin Psychol.* 2019;28:92-101. doi:10.1016/j.copsyc.2018.11.009

6 Zeidan F, Vago DR. Mindfulness meditation-based pain relief: a mechanistic account. *Ann N Y Acad Sci.* 2016;1373(1):114-127. doi:10.1111/nyas.13153 (decreased pain)

7 Bai Z, Chang J, Chen C, Li P, Yang K, Chi I. Investigating the effect of transcendental meditation on blood pressure: a systematic review and meta-analysis. Journal of Human Hypertension 2015 29 :653 – 662.

8 Rosenkranz MA, Lutz A, Perlman DM, et al. Reduced stress and inflammatory responsiveness in experienced meditators compared to a matched healthy control group. *Psychoneuroendocrinology.* 2016;68:117-

125. doi:10.1016/j.psyneuen.2016.02.013

9 Travis F, Valosek L, Konrad A 4th, Link J, Salerno J, Scheller R, Nidich S. Effect of meditation on psychological distress and brain functioning: A randomized controlled study. Brain Cogn. 2018 Aug;125:100-105. doi: 10.1016/j.bandc.2018.03.011. Epub 2018 Jun 21. PMID: 29936408

10 Kabat-Zinn J, Wheeler E, Light T, Skillings A, Scharf MJ, Cropley TG, Hosmer D, Bernhard JD. Influence of a mindfulness meditation-based stress reduction intervention on rates of skin clearing in patients with moderate to severe psoriasis undergoing phototherapy (UVB) and photochemotherapy (PUVA). Psychosom Med. 1998 Sep-Oct;60(5):625-32. doi: 10.1097/00006842-199809000-00020. PMID: 9773769

11 Blase KL, van Waning A. Heart Rate Variability, Cortisol and Attention Focus During Shamatha Quiescence Meditation. Appl Psychophysiol Biofeedback. 2019 Dec;44(4):331-342. doi: 10.1007/s10484-019-09448-w. PMID: 31485894

12 Valosek L, Link J, Mills P, Konrad A, Rainforth M, Nidich S. Effect of Meditation on Emotional Intelligence and Perceived Stress in the Workplace: A Randomized Controlled Study. *Perm J.* 2018;22:17-172. Published 2018 Oct 29. doi:10.7812/TPP/17-172

13 Goyal M, Singh S, Sibinga EMS, et al. Meditation Programs for Psychological Stress and Well-Being [Internet]. Rockville (MD): Agency for Healthcare Research and Quality (US); 2014 Jan. (Comparative Effectiveness Reviews, No. 124.) Available from: https://www.ncbi.nlm.nih.gov/books/NBK180102/

14 Hölzel BK, Carmody J, Vangel M, et al. Mindfulness practice leads to increases in regional brain gray matter density. Psychiatry Res. 2011;191(1):36-43. doi:10.1016/j.pscychresns.2010.08.006

15 Wielgosz J, Goldberg SB, Kral TRA, Dunne JD, Davidson RJ. Mindfulness Meditation and Psychopathology. *Annu Rev Clin Psychol.* 2019;15:285-316. doi:10.1146/annurev-clinpsy-021815-093423999

16 Luders E, Cherbuin N, Kurth F. Forever Young(er): potential age-defying effects of long-term meditation on gray matter atrophy. Front Psychol. 2015 Jan 21;5:1551. doi: 10.3389/fpsyg.2014.01551. PMID: 25653628; PMCID: PMC4300906

CHAPTER 3

WALK AND OTHER FORMS OF EXERCISE

EXERCISE: SUPER STRESS REDUCER

WELCOME TO THE NEXT CORE lifestyle behavior that can enable you to reduce stress, optimize your health, and make you feel great.

"Walk" is the "W" in the Don't Mess With Stress™ system. It encompasses all movement, physical activity, and other forms of exercise, including dance.

Being active improves your health and well-being, which also helps you deal with stress. Exercise releases endorphins and other mediators that calm your body and soul.

Many of you already know how good you feel after a workout, whether that means running, walking, lifting weights, cycling, playing tennis, dancing, or any other physical activity. After exercise, I am often filled with a general sense of happiness and calm, feeling better equipped to face the day. When I use my body, I appreciate it more.

Before industrialization, our ancestors were more physically active. In our current society, we are frequently sedentary, sitting at our desks for hours at a time. When we come home, we tend to sit some more, particularly by watching screens. Prolonged sitting can harm your health. Research has shown that being sedentary increases the risk of obesity, heart disease, stroke, diabetes, and some cancers.[1]

GENERAL BENEFITS OF EXERCISE

Think of exercise as a **health booster** and a **free anti-aging remedy**. Exercise appears to reduce the effect of aging on all our major organ systems.[2] Importantly, it has been shown to decrease "oxidative stress"—a process whereby free radicals and oxidants produced from oxygen metabolism in our cells accumulate to the point where our bodies can no longer clear them. Oxidative stress results from exposure to toxins; e.g., unhealthy food, pollution, negative and harmful thoughts, psychological stress, and radiation.[3] Oxidative stress damages tissues, leaving you vulnerable to many diseases, including cancer, heart disease, rheumatoid arthritis and neurologic diseases such as Parkinson's disease and dementia. Exercise helps you perform your Activities of Daily Living (ADLS) better by improving your ability to lift, lunge, squat, bend, push, and pull.

Research shows that a single bout of any physical activity provides some benefit.[4] Increasing intensity and duration and adding strength and resistance training plus flexibility is the ideal combination in the quest for optimal fitness and well-being. You are building resilience to withstand the rigors of life. A bonus: it improves your appearance. People who exercise have a healthy glow and more muscle mass.

One study showed that a single exercise session improved executive function in the brain, elevated mood, and decreased stress levels.[5]

Here is a list of some of the many proven benefits of exercise. Please note that different benefits result from different forms of exercise.[6]

- Decreased stress.[7]
- Improved balance and fewer falls.[8]
- Improved flexibility.
- Improved muscle strength—prevention of sarcopenia (loss of muscle mass).
- Decreased insulin resistance and decreased risk of Type 2 diabetes.
- Decreased aging by lengthening telomeres (the caps on the ends of chromosomes).
- Improved mood and reduced depression.[9]

- Decreased anxiety.[10]
- Improved memory and brain functioning.
- Improved immunity.
- Improved diversity of the gut microbiome—a good thing.
- Increases BDNF—Brain Derived Neurotrophic Factor—which stimulates brain neurons to grow.
- Increases endorphins—the "feel good" hormones.
- Lowered blood pressure.[11]
- Improved sleep.
- Relief from constipation.[12]

TYPE, DURATION, AND INTENSITY

What type of exercise is best for reducing stress? There is ongoing research dedicated to what constitutes the minimum and at what point there is no additional benefit. The general consensus appears to be that you will benefit from any form of physical activity and movement. However, the best benefits in terms of stress reduction come from moderate activity. High intensity exercise can actually add to stress in some people.[13] Know your own limits.

Do what you can! Start by taking breaks from all the sitting. Get up and move for about 5 to 10 minutes every half hour to an hour.

The American Heart Association recommends the following exercise prescription:

- 150 minutes per week of moderate aerobic activity or 75 minutes of somewhat more intense activity. For the best results, combine the two and not just on the weekends. Weekend warriors are much more likely to be injured.
- Two days per week, add moderate to intense resistance or weight training to increase muscle strength.
- Sit less! Just walking around the house or up and down the stairs helps mitigate the effects of being sedentary. Consider a standing desk. Sitting on a stability ball can help with core strength—but take care not to let your posture suffer.
- Want more benefits? Increase your exercise to five hours per week and increase frequency and intensity over time.

Your goals? To improve the functioning of your heart and lungs, to strengthen muscles and improve endurance, to increase flexibility, and to improve your Body Mass Index (BMI)—in other words, lower your body fat. Ideally you would combine different exercises that address all these physical goals. According to fitness trainer Ingrid Tarjan, all exercise programs should include a variation of 7 Core Moves—Push, Pull, Carry, Squat, Hinge, Lunge, and Rotate. Some of you may be shaking your heads. Yes, the prospect of such a significant change in your routine can be overwhelming, so start with a workout that is realistic for you.

If you haven't been exercising and you have health risk factors such as being overweight, high cholesterol, heart disease, diabetes, kidney disease, or cancer, it is important to consult your doctor before starting any exercise program. Never just dive into an exercise regime. To avoid injury, start by warming up the muscles slowly and end with a cool-down.

Walking as the Core of Your Workout

Walking is so good for your body. It can decrease the risk of dementia, Type 2 diabetes, heart disease, depression, and the pain of arthritis. It's a great place to start and it's also an excellent aerobic exercise. Begin with a short distance, such as a half a block. You don't have to walk quickly. Just walk. If that is too much, do less. Try to slowly increase the distance.

For greater benefits, increase the intensity, duration, and frequency. Add steps or a hill. You can break up your walking workout into 5 or 10 minutes at a time. Do this 3 times per day and you have walked 30 minutes!

THE 10,000 STEPS PER DAY "RULE"

The 10,000 steps per day rule seems to harken back to a product first sold in Japan in the mid-1960s. Manpo-kei stands for "10,000 steps meter." So that amount, which most people assume is set in stone, was determined by a marketing tool! Dr. I-Min Lee from Harvard Medical School did a study to see if 10,000 steps really affected your mortality—that is, would it make you live longer—and whether the intensity of the steps mattered. Her conclusion: to lower your chance of an early death, you need not walk more than 7,500 steps per day (as measured on your smartphone or activity tracker). Intensity didn't matter. However, this study did NOT focus on the number of steps needed to affect the quality of our lives, reduce dementia, or help prevent physical illness.

Here are Dr. Lee's recommendations.

- Choose the stairs, not the elevator.
- Choose the open parking space farthest from the entrance.
- Taking the bus or subway? Exit before your stop for extra walking time.
- Doing chores? Let's say you're bringing the laundry upstairs. Aim for more trips up and down the stairs rather than fewer.

"Those little things collectively add up," Dr. Lee

says. "Don't be intimidated or dissuaded by the 10,000 number."[14]

STEP UP YOUR EXERCISE

After you have kept up your Walk routine for at least a week, I recommend that—as long as you have no medical contraindications to moderate intensity or vigorous exercise—you follow the American Heart Association Guidelines. Try to make movement fun. You could enlist a friend or partner to exercise with you. Thanks to the Pandemic, there are many more online exercise classes to choose from.

What constitutes moderate intensity exercise? Here are some examples adapted from the advice of Christopher Travers, an exercise physiologist at the Cleveland Clinic:

ONLY HAVE 15-20 MINUTES? DO ONE OF THE FOLLOWING:

- Run 1½ miles
- Jump rope
- Walk stairs
- Swim Laps
- Shoot hoops

30 MINUTES

- Walk 2 miles

- Bike 5 miles
- Do water aerobics
- Rake leaves
- Dance

45 MINUTES
- Play volleyball, tennis, pickleball, or badminton
- Wash your car
- Garden
- Rake leaves

So far we've only covered low-tech ways to exercise. In 2006, the home video console Wii revolutionized home exercise. By 2017, it had been discontinued due to competition from the Nintendo Switch. Wii is still out there, along with many fun alternatives if you can afford to invest in some new software and a game console. What about virtual reality (VR) games? From Fitness Boxing to Ring Fit Adventure, you can turn your living room into a boxing ring, an '80s disco, or a country road. A simple internet search reveals a wealth of **high-tech options** that can entertain you while helping you get fit.

YOUR TARGET HEART RATE

When exercising, we aim for a target heart rate. According to the American Heart Association, you can easily determine your target heart rates. You first determine your maximum heart rate, which is 220 minus your age. For example, for a 50-year-old person, the maximum heart rate would be 220-50=170. To calculate the target heart rate during moderate intensity exercise, multiply your maximum heart rate (170) times 50 to 70%. A 50-year-old person exercising moderately on the lower end would have a target heart rate of 85, (170 times 0.50). For more strenuous exercise, multiply the maximum heart rate x 70 to 85%. The same 50-year-old exercising strenuously would have a target heart rate of 0.85 of 170, or 145.

You can find your heart rate if you have fitness tracker, or you can get your pulse the old-fashioned way on the inner side of your wrist or in the neck. I recommend using the wrist, because pressing too hard on the vessels in your neck could possibly make you pass out.

The pulse you find at the wrist is called the radial pulse. Turn your hand over so the palm is showing. With the index and middle fingers of your other hand (not the thumb), feel the pulsation on the wrist on the thumb side. Look at a watch or set a timer for 15 seconds. Count the number of pulsations over 15 seconds and multiply that by 4. I recommend visiting the Centers for Disease Control and Prevention (CDC)[15] website for more information.

You can also use the **"talk" test**. For moderate exercise, you should be able to talk—though it will be more difficult than usual—but not sing. For vigorous exercise, you'll only be able to manage a few words.

DANCE TO MAKE EXERCISE FUN

World-renown ballet dancer Jacques d'Amboise founded the National Dance Institute to promote dancing as both an art form and a means of self-expression and exercise. He introduced school children all over the world to dance. He famously said, "Dance is your pulse, your heartbeat, your breathing. A wild, untamed youth learns nobility through art."

Some people don't think of dance as exercise. Research has shown that it produces the same benefits, possibly more.[16]

Dancing improves our well-being in many ways, from decreased stress to improved cardiovascular fitness, brain health, memory, and mood, as well as increased flexibility. When done with a partner or in a group, it can create social connection. And learning new choreography helps build new brain connections and enhance neuroplasticity.

A 2018 study[17] showed that learning complicated dance moves increased brain volumes in more areas as compared to a conventional fitness program, and the people doing the dancing had increased levels of BDNF—the protein that promotes the growth and survival of new neurons.

The great thing about dancing is that you can do it at home, freestyle, while no one is watching. You can also receive formal training in ballet, modern dance, or ballroom dancing—to name a few dance forms. Take classes online. Let the music move you both emotionally as well as physically.

So, if you don't like to jog or run or go to the gym, dancing might be just the thing. You'll have fun while you exercise, get healthier, and release stress.

STARTING YOUR EXERCISE PROGRAM

Like anything else you undertake, you must take that first step, and in this case, that is a literal step. Remember to first get clearance from your physician. Then, if feasible, consult with a personal trainer or sign up for online classes. You want to make sure that you protect yourself from injury.

Next, you will need to motivate yourself to start and continue to exercise. When making a lifestyle change, it is important to decide WHY you are making this change. The WHY will get you through those times when you don't want to exercise.

Here is an "exercise" that will help. (Again, no pun intended!)

Write down 3 reasons WHY you should start moving. Maybe you'd like to look great in an outfit, feel younger, or make your son proud at his wedding. Remember, you'll also be optimizing your bone health, heart health, brain health, musculoskeletal health and flexibility, and your ability to perform the Activities of Daily Living (ADLS). A comprehensive-enough WHY will motivate you to start an exercise program and continue even when every bone in your body is telling you to give up.

ACTION STEPS

Start by setting goals. Writing them in the present tense is more powerful.

- I walk 10 blocks in one week.
- My waist circumference is now xx inches.
- I am much less stressed and reactive.
- By (pick a date), I have lost 5 pounds.

On your calendar, schedule the times you will be doing the exercises that will best help you achieve these goals. Visualize and imagine how good you will look and feel after these goals have been met. Reward yourself for achieving your goals. Take a hot bath with healing bath salts. Ordinarily, I would recommend treating yourself to a massage, but that might not be wise during the Pandemic.

Start slow and make sure to do things correctly so you don't hurt yourself. If your goal is to lose weight, remember that gradual weight loss is the only kind that lasts. Muscle weighs more than fat, so you may even find that your improved physique does not necessarily result in very different numbers on the scale.

If the prospect of a consistent exercise regime leaves you stymied, start small. Think of Dr. Lee's recommendations. Get off the bus one stop earlier. Take 5 to 10-minute breaks from sitting at your desk each hour to walk around and stretch. Walk up a flight of stairs instead of taking the elevator if it is safe for you to do. These small chunks of movement add up. Break down a 30-minute walk into 3 increments of 10 minutes per day, and you have achieved your daily goal!

If you like to measure things, I recommend wearing a fitness tracker to see how many steps you are getting per day. Or use the built-in app on your smartphone to check your steps and stairs. If you don't reach a goal, don't let it discourage you. Congratulate yourself for what you have accomplished and aim to reach your goal next time.

Writing your goals and commitments down in a calendar or in the notes section of your phone increases the chances that you will actually do them. This applies to all of the Don't Mess With Stress™ recommendations.

After you have incorporated more physical activity into your life, jot down or make a mental note of how you feel. Pay particular attention to the benefits. Has your mood improved? Do your clothes fit better?

Once you start moving, you may want to expand your repertoire by adding other forms of aerobic exercise and incorporate strength training:

- Ride a stationary bike and/or bike outside.
- Find a personal trainer to recommend strength training, stretching and flexibility exercises that are safe for you.
- Buy weights and start a strength-training routine.

Weight training can also increase bone density.[18]

- Add exercises to improve your balance and prevent falls. Keeping your muscles working will help you to retain muscle mass as you age.

In closing, I'd like to re-state my core beliefs about physical activity. I believe that keeping your body flexible carries over to life in general, making you more flexible when it comes to human interactions and challenging situations, especially stressful ones. Exercise helps build resilience and makes you look and feel vital and healthy.

Remember: it starts with one step. Just taking a stroll for 30 minutes twice per day can lower blood pressure.[19]

Have fun and try to do some form of movement every day, even if it's only dancing in your pajamas in the morning. Toward that goal, I'd like to share a fun dance I created to stimulate your brain and heart and improve your mood.

THE DON'T MESS WITH STRESS™ DANCE

You can do this dance while walking down the sidewalk or marching in your house.

Say the words, "Diet, Meditate, Walk, and Sleep" while you do the choreography with your hands and arms.

- **Diet:** using one hand, touch your index finger to

your thumb and move them toward your mouth.

- **Meditate:** both hands, index fingers touching thumbs with palms up.
- **Walk:** arms swinging, as if you are running.
- **Sleep:** palms together raised on angle toward left side of face.

While walking or marching in place, say the phrase, "Diet, Meditate, Walk, and Sleep" three times using the hand positions, then point your thumb at your heart and say, "Me, Me." Finally, say, "We" and hold out your hands, palms up. The "Me" refers to taking care of yourself and the "We" to working together to make the world a better place.

Welcome to a stronger, more resilient you!

Endnotes

1   Ekelund U, Steene-Johannessen J, Brown WJ, Fagerland MW, Owen N, Powell KE, Bauman A, Lee IM; Lancet Physical Activity Series 2 Executive Committee; Lancet Sedentary Behaviour Working Group. Does physical activity attenuate, or even eliminate, the detrimental association of sitting time with mortality? A harmonised meta-analysis of data from more than 1 million men and women. Lancet. 2016 Sep 24;388(10051):1302-10. doi: 10.1016/S0140-6736(16)30370-1. Epub 2016 Jul 28. Erratum in: Lancet. 2016 Sep 24;388(10051):e6. PMID: 27475271.

2   Garatachea N, Pareja-Galeano H, Sanchis-Gomar F, Santos-Lozano A, Fiuza-Luces C, Morán M, Emanuele E, Joyner MJ, Lucia A. Exercise attenuates the major hallmarks of aging. Rejuvenation Res. 2015 Feb;18(1):57-89. doi: 10.1089/rej.2014.1623. PMID: 25431878; PMCID: PMC4340807.

3   Aschbacher K, O'Donovan A, Wolkowitz OM, Dhabhar FS, Su Y, Epel E. Good stress, bad stress and oxidative stress: insights from anticipatory cortisol reactivity. Psychoneuroendocrinology. 2013 Sep;38(9):1698-708. doi: 10.1016/j.psyneuen.2013.02.004. Epub 2013 Mar 13. PMID: 23490070; PMCID: PMC4028159.

4   The Effects of Acute Exercise on Mood, Cognition, Neurophysiology, and Neurochemical Pathways: A Review. Julia C. Basso and Wendy A. Suzuki *Brain Plast. 2017; 2(2): 127–152.

5   Warburton DE, Nicol CW, Bredin SS. Health benefits of physical activity: the evidence. *CMAJ. 2006;174(6):801-809. doi:10.1503/cmaj.051351*

6   Nieman DC, Wentz LM. The compelling link between physical activity and the body's defense system. J Sport Health Sci. 2019 May;8(3):201-217. doi: 10.1016/j.jshs.2018.09.009. Epub 2018 Nov 16. PMID: 31193280; PMCID: PMC6523821.

7   Puterman E, Weiss J, Lin J, Schilf S, Slusher AL, Johansen KL, Epel ES. Aerobic exercise lengthens telomeres and reduces stress in family caregivers: A randomized controlled trial - Curt Richter Award Paper 2018. Psychoneuroendocrinology. 2018 Dec;98:245-252. doi: 10.1016/j.psyneuen.2018.08.002. Epub 2018 Aug 2. PMID: 30266522.

8   Sherrington C, Fairhall NJ, Wallbank GK, et al. Exercise for preventing falls in older people living in the community. *Cochrane Database Syst Rev.* 2019;1(1):CD012424. Published 2019 Jan 31. doi:10.1002/14651858.CD012424.pub2.

9   Dinas PC, Koutedakis Y, Flouris AD. Effects of exercise and physical activity on depression. Ir J Med Sci. 2011 Jun;180(2):319-25. doi: 10.1007/s11845-010-0633-9. Epub 2010 Nov 14. PMID: 21076975.

10 Chen YC, Chen C, Martínez RM, Etnier JL, Cheng Y. Habitual physical activity mediates the acute exercise-induced modulation of anxiety-related amygdala functional connectivity. Sci Rep. 2019 Dec

24;9(1):19787. doi: 10.1038/s41598-019-56226-z. PMID: 31875047; PMCID: PMC6930267.

11 Boutcher YN, Boutcher SH. Exercise intensity and hypertension: what's new? J Hum Hypertens. 2017 Mar;31(3):157-164. doi: 10.1038/jhh.2016.62. Epub 2016 Sep 8. PMID: 27604656.

12 Rong Huang, Sai-Yin Ho, Wing-Sze Lo, Tai-Hing Lam. Physical Activity and Constipation in Hong Kong Adolescents PLoS One. 2014; 9(2): e90193.

13 Paolucci EM, Loukov D, Bowdish DME, Heisz JJ. Exercise reduces depression and inflammation but intensity matters. Biol Psychol. 2018 Mar;133:79-84. doi: 10.1016/j.biopsycho.2018.01.015. Epub 2018 Feb 3. PMID: 29408464.

14 health.harvard.edu/blog/10000-steps-a-day-or-fewer-2019071117305.

15 https://www.cdc.gov/physicalactivity/basics/measuring/heartrate.htm

16 Kim S, Kim J. Mood after Various Brief Exercise and Sport Modes: Aerobics, Hip-Hop Dancing, ICE Skating, and Body Conditioning. *Perceptual and Motor Skills*. 2007;104(3_suppl):1265-1270. doi:10.2466/pms.104.4.1265-1270

17 Rehfeld K, Lüders A, Hökelmann A, Lessmann V, Kaufmann J, Brigadski T, Müller P, Müller NG. Dance training is superior to repetitive physical exercise in inducing brain plasticity in the elderly. PLoS One. 2018 Jul 11;13(7):e0196636. doi: 10.1371/journal.pone.0196636. PMID: 29995884; PMCID: PMC6040685.

18 Watson SL, Weeks BK, Weis LJ, Harding AT, Horan SA, Beck BR. High-Intensity Resistance and Impact Training Improves Bone Mineral Density and Physical Function in Postmenopausal Women With Osteopenia and Osteoporosis: The LIFTMOR Randomized Controlled Trial. J Bone Miner Res. 2018 Feb;33(2):211-220. doi: 10.1002/jbmr.3284. Epub 2017 Oct 4. Erratum in: J Bone Miner Res. 2019 Mar;34(3):572. PMID: 28975661.

19 Lu Q, Wang SM, Liu YX, et al. Low-intensity walking as mild medication for pressure control in prehypertensive and hypertensive subjects: how far shall we wander?. *Acta Pharmacol Sin.* 2019;40(8):1119-1126. doi:10.1038/s41401-018-0202-8.

CHAPTER 4

THE QUEST FOR A GOOD NIGHT'S SLEEP

SLEEP, YOU, AND THE HUMAN RACE

SLEEP IS ONE OF THE cornerstones and foundations of the Don't Mess With Stress!™ system. Without quality sleep, you'll lack energy, vitality, and enthusiasm for life. As we face an uncertain future overshadowed by a pandemic, stress and anxiety are seriously disrupting our sleeping hours.

The information and suggestions in this chapter will empower you to address your sleep issues head on. But first, an overview. Why is sleep so important? What are its benefits? What causes sleeplessness? What are the consequences of sleep deprivation? And finally, what can we do to improve our sleep duration and quality? Feeling rested after a good night's sleep will also make you a nicer person to be around, allowing you to be an ambassador of kindness in the world. Let's add some levity and fun to this challenging situation.

YOU ARE NOT ALONE

Realizing the importance of a good night's sleep can inspire you to develop good sleep habits. Millions of people—1 in 4 Americans—have sleep issues and insomnia. These range from the challenges of maintaining a regular bedtime routine, to falling asleep, staying asleep, and getting back to sleep after waking during the night. Lack of adequate sleep takes its toll on physical, mental, and emotional health. The resulting irritability and agitation can negatively impact those around us. The good news is that 75%[1] of people with insomnia recover.

I know firsthand what sleep deprivation feels like. I had the most extreme and consistent sleep deficit during my residency training, the time when I was learning how to practice medicine. I was on call every third night. That meant I might be up all night and then have to stay awake the whole next day to perform my duties in the hospital. I remember driving home and barely being able to keep my eyes on the road. This is unhealthy, dangerous, and paradoxical to what we preach in medicine in terms of sleep habits.

Things have gotten better since I trained. Today's interns and residents typically get to go home the next day after being on call. Still, I'm guessing they still have major sleep deficits.

Since my residency, I have intermittently experienced different types of sleep issues. I sometimes have trouble falling asleep, and I occasionally wake up in the night and can't get back to sleep. Following a poor night's sleep, I feel irritable and less efficient at tasks. I have decreased attention and focus and a strong desire to find a place to lie down. I discovered that I was grinding my teeth while I slept, probably from stress. In fact, the pressure from the grinding was so great, I broke some teeth. I got a nightguard, which helped with the grinding and relieved some of the tension on my facial muscles. This intervention, however, didn't help with the fatigue I felt after a full night's sleep.

After a prolonged period of waking up poorly rested, I decided to consult a sleep physician. I had a sleep study done. The cause of my interrupted sleep remained unclear, though they did rule out sleep apnea. The sleep specialist advised me to create a bedtime routine that included stopping screens an hour before bed and to go to bed and wake up at regular hours.

By applying the sleep specialist's recommendations and the techniques I lay out in this chapter, I have greatly improved my sleep quality and duration. I confess that at times I still have trouble shutting down my screens and committing to a regular bedtime. However, I continue to work on my sleep "hygiene" because I know how important sleep is for my brain and body.

WHY IS SLEEP SO IMPORTANT?

Despite years of research, we still don't fully understand why sleep is necessary and what it does for our bodies and minds. There are many theories. As Mathew Walker, PhD, says in his excellent book, *Why We Sleep*, "We sleep for a rich litany of functions, plural—an abundant constellation of nighttime benefits that service both our brains and our bodies." Dr. Walker believes there is a global sleep deficit. Just imagine the negative impact on the well-being of our world because of sleep deprivation. Dr. Walker argues for making the subject of sleep awareness important enough in our schools that it will be passed down through the generations.

According to Dr. Walker, poor sleep can make you sick and cause you to die early. These are not happy facts! The good news, which we'll explore later in this chapter, is that you can do something about it.

Sleep has so many benefits. It gives our bodies a chance to renew themselves. During sleep we heal faster, and in the morning, we find ourselves better able to face difficulties or solve problems. If you memorize something before bed, the way that information is processed in your sleep will make it more likely to stay with you. It is a time for our brains to sort through and discard information and experiences and our bodies to work their restorative magic.

Nan Lu, OMD, a Traditional Chinese Medicine expert,

states that the one thing you can do for yourself that is more important than food, exercise, Tai Chi, Qi Gong, etc. is SLEEP. It's free and it gives us dreams, which can provide insight into our souls and possibly even our health issues.

THE HAZARDS OF SLEEP DEPRIVATION

Quality sleep improves our mental, physical, and emotional functioning, including our metabolisms, hearts, and immune systems. You name it, sleep affects it. In fact, a chronic lack of quality sleep can have dire or even tragic results. Below are some of the consequences of inadequate sleep:

- **Poor decision making**. If we haven't slept well, we are more apt to be impulsive. Studies of sleep-deprived athletes, soldiers, and pilots all bear this out. And certainly, we have all experienced it.
- **Increased risk of accidents**. Studies[2] show that being sleep-deprived can impair your driving as much as being legally intoxicated. You are more likely to stumble and fall, more likely to burn yourself cooking—all accidents that can be avoided if you get your proper rest.
- **Memory impairment**. Whether it's learning a new skill or procedure or recalling your dialogue in a play, sufficient sleep is what consolidates[3] these memories.

- **Immune dysfunction**. Without sleep you are much more likely to get sick—everything from a common cold, to COVID-19, a chronic disease, diabetes, cancer, or Alzheimer's.
- **Weight gain and diabetes**. Lack of sleep creates hormone imbalances, making you hungrier and less likely to feel full. It also affects blood sugar levels, making you more likely to develop diabetes.
- **Increased sensitivity to pain**. In one study,[4] even healthy people deprived of sleep were less tolerant of cold and heat, more bothered by intense pressure.
- **Anxiety and depression**. Research[5] has confirmed that sleep is important to staying on an even keel. Without a decent night's sleep, you are more likely to overreact to bad news and under-react to good news.
- **Accelerated Aging**. An April 2019 study[6] showed that sleep apnea (disrupted sleep caused by snoring and other factors) increases our biological age—the age our organs and cells indicate rather than our chronological age.

What Causes Insomnia?

Now that we have a better idea of the importance of sleep, it's crucial to find out WHY we have problems sleeping.

Many factors affect sleep. Your mental or emotional state, for one. Some medical conditions cause you to sleep too much, others to sleep too little. You might have a vitamin deficiency or there might be too much noise or light in your environment. Perhaps you need a more comfortable mattress, sheets, or pillow.

Ask yourself, do any of these issues apply to you?

- You are exposing yourself to **blue light** at bedtime, either from your phone or computer.
- You have **sleep apnea**, a condition by which you stop breathing several times during the night.
- You have digestive issues, such as Gastroesophageal Reflux Disease (GERD), that make you cough, choke, or wake up suddenly.
- You **obsess** about your problems and worries.
- Your sleep is interrupted by frequent **bathroom breaks**.
- You have **nightmares** or walk in your sleep.
- You drink coffee or tea or eat chocolate (also a source of **caffeine**) too close to bedtime.
- You drink too much **alcohol**, which after initially helping you fall asleep causes you to wake frequently during the night.
- You **exercise in the evening**, which may leave you overstimulated.
- You take **medications** that interfere with sleep.
- You **grind** your teeth.

- **Your partner** snores or has restless leg syndrome.
- You have **jet lag**.
- You have a **Vitamin D deficiency**.
- Your sleep is disrupted by **electromagnetic radiation** due to phones, screens, or an alarm clock.
- Your mattress and/or pillow are **uncomfortable**.

As you can see, there are many factors that can lead to sleep problems. Identifying and correcting these issues will definitely improve your sleep, health, and well-being. In many cases, the answer is "Just don't do it," but of course it is never that simple.

If after considering this list, you are still stymied, then consider consulting a sleep specialist—one who is also a medical doctor. Many hospitals now have Sleep Centers. It is important to first rule out organic problems such as sleep apnea. If, after further evaluation with a medical sleep specialist you are told there are no physical or anatomical causes for your sleep issues, then you should seek out a psychologist or other specialist to learn cognitive behavioral skills that pertain specifically to sleep.

Read on for some suggestions to get you started on sleeping better.

IMPROVING YOUR SLEEP HYGIENE

A simple examination of your own sleep environment

may help. Perhaps there is an easy fix, such as wearing earplugs or noise-canceling headphones, donning a sleep mask, or installing black-out blinds. A new pillow might work wonders.

Establish a **Pre-Bedtime Routine**. A pilot does a preflight check before taking off, an athlete does a muscle warm-up, and a singer goes through a series of vocalizations. Like them, you can take extra steps to ensure that your undertaking—in this case, an excellent night's sleep—will be a success.

The time before bed should be designed to help you "wind down" and prepare your body for sleep. Here is a "pre-bedtime" check list to help you on your way to a great night's sleep.

- At least one hour before bedtime, **move your electronic devices**, ideally to another room, or if not, at least 10 feet from your bed with screens turned off. Blue light decreases melatonin and interferes with Rapid Eye Movement (REM) sleep and can even damage the eyes.[7] If you enjoy reading before bed, do it in another room and either read an actual book or a Kindle with front light or a Kindle Paperwhite. These do not omit significant amounts of blue light because the LEDs are directed toward the page, not your eyes. There are ways to make tablets less stimulating, though you are still better off avoiding them completely in the hour before bed. The Kindle Fire features a blue light filtering mode called "Blue Shade" that Amazon claims reduces blue light exposure. The Kindle Oasis has "adjustable warm light." The iPad has a "Night Shift" feature. Blue-light glasses may also help.

- Aim to **go to bed at the same time** every night, ideally before 11 p.m., even on weekends. Going to bed after midnight disturbs your circadian rhythms, meaning that you won't get the full benefits of your sleep cycles. You may think you're a night owl, but the light outside is telling your body something else. Even if your schedule allows you to sleep in, your neighbors and even the birds and animals will conspire to wake you up earlier.

- Aim to **wake at the same time** each morning. Ideally you won't need an alarm clock because you will be well rested, and your body will be conditioned to wake up at that time. Most of us need 7-9 hours of sleep. Alarm clocks can be jolting, but if you need one, don't use the snooze button.

- Make sure that your **bedroom is dark enough**. Look for extraneous light sources that may be disturbing your sleep. You may need blackout blinds or shades if you live in the city or have a neighbor with outdoor lighting. Consider a sleep mask, which can also soothe dry eyes.

- Is your bedroom **cool enough**? According to the National Sleep Foundation, the optimum bedroom temperature should be 60 to 67 degrees Fahrenheit.

- Before going to bed, **take a hot bath**, listen to relaxing music, or read something reassuring and not stimulating enough to keep you up. Save your thrillers and page-turners for daytime. Add Epsom Salts to your bath. They contain magnesium that is absorbed into the skin and can be very calming.

- Try **aromatherapy**. In a 2017 Study,[8] lavender oil was shown to reduce anxiety and improved sleep quality.

- Your bedroom should be for **sleep or sexual activity only**. Using that room for other activities, such as watching TV, working on your laptop, or reading will make you associate bed with those activities.

- **Think twice before exercising in the evening**. An October 2018 study published in *Sports Medicine* says it's okay to exercise in the evening as long as you stop one hour before bed, but your personal experience may tell you otherwise.

Problems Falling Asleep or Falling Back to Sleep

Nothing works for everyone. Your task—a pleasurable one, I hope—will be to find the tool or tools that work for you at those times when you can't fall asleep or find yourself fully awake in the middle of the night. Sometimes one tool can make all the difference. But you may require a full toolshed to adapt to changes in your physiology, state of mind, and the season.

- After 20 minutes of sleeplessness, **go to another room** and engage in an activity that is relaxing for you. Knitting, reading a slow-paced novel, sniffing some lavender oil. Resist the temptation to look at your screens.
- **Cognitive Behavioral Therapy (CBT)** is a well-established technique to treat anxiety and depression. It teaches you how to avoid "unhelpful" thinking that solves nothing and increases stress; e.g., mulling over past events or traumas, castigating yourself for selfish or worse behavior, and obsessing over facts that cannot be changed. If you can identify your personal tripping points, you will be better able to identify and disregard this kind of negative thinking when it plagues you in the middle of the night. How does CBT apply directly to sleep? It challenges

one's beliefs about sleep and replaces them with more empowering beliefs. **Cognitive Behavioral Therapy for Insomnia (CBT-I)** can consist of a series of one-to-one sessions, but there are also apps you can download. One free app is called CBT-I Coach. Developed by the Veterans Administration, Stanford University and the Department of Defense, it has evidence-based scientific research showing its effectiveness.[9] It is available for the public on App Stores. I have used it and found it to be easy to use and helpful to manage my insomnia.

- **What about counting sheep**? Maybe. According to Sydney sleep psychologist Dianne Richards, it's best to choose images that are "very simple, very repetitive and somewhat boring." That might entail examining a picture in your head or recalling a beautiful place you have visited in detail. Think of it as a mental screensaver. Maybe you're just watching bubbles float by or water rippling. A creek moving over rocks.

A FEW ANECDOTAL SUGGESTIONS FROM FRIENDS, COLLEAGUES, PATIENTS, ETC.:

- "Warm milk still does it for me."
- "I relax every part of my body starting with my toes. I'm often asleep before I get to my head."

- "I breathe as deeply and slowly as possible, concentrating wholly on this process."
- "If I wake up from a nightmare, I try to reframe the dream until the outcome is positive or I get up and move around until I have fully accepted that it's a dream, then read something soothing."
- "I move into another room and do some gentle stretching exercises."
- "I listen to soothing music."

MEDICATIONS, TEAS, AND SUPPLEMENTS FOR ANXIETY AND INSOMNIA

First, it is important to note that herbs and supplements can have side effects and interactions with pharmaceutical medications, other herbs, and food. I recommend taking them only under the guidance of your health provider.

Avoid prescription or over-the-counter sleep medications if possible. They have side effects—some can even make you walk, drive, and eat in your sleep—and you may become addicted. Many people use over-the-counter antihistamines such as Benadryl, the brand name for the generic diphenhydramine, to help them sleep. Don't. You may eventually develop a tolerance, and side effects include dry mouth, problems urinating, and constipation.

There are several herbs, teas, and supplements known for their ability to calm us down and help us sleep. Consult a health practitioner about the best herbs for you, and take care not to mix them with alcohol, antidepressants, or other commercial or prescription sleep remedies. If your physician is fine with you trying one or more of these supplements and they work for you, they are unlikely to harm you.

- **Melatonin** is a sleep hormone that increases at bedtime. The supplement can help you fall asleep faster and enjoy better quality sleep. It can be especially useful for people who need to re-set their body's sleep clock due to odd work hours or jet lag. Choose the synthetic form, because the type made from the pineal gland of animals might carry viruses. Start at a low dose, such as 0.5mg (not 5mg), and increase the dose as necessary. Melatonin is not recommended if you are taking certain medications, such as anticoagulants.
- **Chamomile** calms you down and helps you sleep, but it also has healing properties and is good for the gut.
- **Peppermint** and **ginger** aid in digestion, and mint tea relaxes and heals.
- **Passionflower tea** is prescribed to treat insomnia, nerves, and anxiety. One study found that it is as effective as the prescription drug oxazepam as an anxiety treatment.[10]

- **Valerian root** helps you calm down and sleep, but don't rely on it for longer than a month to avoid side effects. Do not take it with alcohol because the level of sedation might be harmful. It can also interact negatively with medicine and other herbs, among them acetaminophen (Tylenol), estrogens, oral contraceptives, and many different herbs.

- **L-theanine**, contained in black and green teas, can improve mood, attention span, and memory. If you are sensitive to caffeine, green tea is lower but drinking too much of either could interfere with sleep.

- **Magnesium**, one of the most important minerals in the body, tends to decrease as we age. It is involved in many biochemical reactions in the body. Research[11] has shown that taking Magnesium can help insomnia. The ideal dose is not clear. I would recommend starting with 200mg of Magnesium Oxide. Magnesium oxide is usually the cheapest form. There are many magnesium supplements, including Magnesium Glycinate and Magnesium Citrate. Magnesium Oxide and Magnesium Citrate could cause loose stools if taken in higher doses. As with any of my recommendations, you should not take magnesium without speaking with your doctor or health provider, especially if you have heart or kidney issues.

Action Steps

Knowing WHY you want to change a behavior is one of the key factors that help you make new habits and stick to them. The following are action steps that may improve your sleep.

- **Create your Why**. Write down 3 key reasons why it is important to get quality sleep; e.g., you want to look younger, slow down aging, and improve your memory.
- **Start with baby steps**. If you usually go to bed after midnight, try going to bed one hour earlier than your regular bedtime for a few days. If that works for you, then keep moving your bedtime back every few days until you are in bed sometime before midnight.
- **Keep a gratitude journal** to put you in a positive frame of mind before bed. Write down 3 to 5 reasons for being grateful. Feel this gratitude in your body.
- **Create a game around sleep**. Find a friend who is also having a sleep issue and share progress and failures. Empower each other to create bedtime rituals—closing down screens, winding down, taking a bath, writing down gratitude, celebrating the day's accomplishments.
- **Challenge yourself in a gentle and fun way**. See how many days in a row you can be in bed

by a designated time. Make it a game and reward yourself if you reach your goal. If you don't reach your goal, then tell yourself you will do better next time. No need for punishment. Make this fun!

- **Laugh!** Laughter relaxes the body. Watch a funny video or a comedian on YouTube one to two hours before bedtime. Read a funny book. Laughing increases endorphins, relaxes muscles, and enhances well-being.[12]
- **Get a massage** or give one.
- **Try reflexology**. Massaging certain pressure points on the feet, hands, and ears benefits your organs and other body parts that respond to those points.
- **Be kind to yourself**. If you don't sleep well one night, the world won't end. Simply by being in bed you are getting some rest.
- **Have sex**. (With or without a partner).
- **Avoid heavy meals within 3 hours of bedtime**. If you are hungry, a light snack at bedtime such as warm milk or cheese and crackers may help you sleep because milk and cheese contain tryptophan, which can stimulate sleep hormones. A piece of toast topped with almond butter and banana slices is one of the snacks recommended by Sleep.org. Some breakfast cereals are also enriched with tryptophan. If you suffer from Gastroesophageal

Reflux (GERD), you should ideally avoid eating for 3 hours before bedtime.

- **Do not use tobacco**, which is a stimulant and harmful in so many other ways.

- **Avoid alcohol** 3-4 hours before bedtime. Alcohol can wake you up several times a night and block REM sleep (the time when we dream). As Dr. Matthew Walker says, "sedation is not sleep."

- **Don't use marijuana**. Like alcohol, marijuana blocks REM sleep, and lack of REM sleep can make you more anxious.

- **Don't use CBD Oil** as a sleep aid. The research for sleep and CBD—a cannabinoid without THC that does not make you high—is still in its infancy. There are currently no official recommendations I am aware of for dosage of CBD for insomnia. There are also concerns about adverse reactions to CBD[13] as well as potential for interactions with other drugs,[14] as well as the development of tolerance to CBD. It is best to consult your physician before taking CBD.

- **Avoid napping during the daytime**, especially if you have difficulty falling asleep at night.

- **Exercise!** Physical fatigue helps counteract emotional fatigue.

- **Do not clock-watch**. It will make you more anxious.

- **No pets in the bedroom**, unless they relax you and don't disrupt your sleep. For more information on this subject, check out this article by the American Kennel Club.[15]
- **Read *Why We Sleep: Unlocking the Power of Sleep and Dreams*** by Matthew Walker, PhD, or listen to one of his excellent talks on YouTube.

Online Sleep Resources

To quote the "About Us" page on its website, **SleepFoundation.org**, the National Sleep Foundation "features a medical board, expanded sleep science coverage, data-driven content, consumer reports, and intensive reviews of different sleep and wellness products."

Here are three other websites that offer advice for choosing sleep products but also provide easily understood descriptions of the sleep cycle and offer comprehensive lists of treatments and therapies both conventional and alternative.

- **Tuck.com**. "Sleep products are our passion." They "research, analyze, and test every product that impacts sleep."
- **BetterSleep.org**. "With an unbiased voice, the BSC [Better Sleep Council] is comprised of bedding leaders and sleep experts who represent

a cross-section of the mattress industry."

- **Sleep.org** "feature[s] commercial product reviews and consumer guides along with the expert sleep health and science content you've come to expect."

A GOOD NIGHT'S SLEEP IS IN YOUR FUTURE

At this point, you may be feeling overwhelmed by all the information you've absorbed. As with all the tools provided in the DMWS system, don't take on too much all at once.

Here is one great example of how changing just one sleep habit can make a dramatic difference in your health. One of my patients—a highly stressed and ambitious young man in his early twenties I'll call Corey—came to me complaining of fatigue. I reviewed his bloods and found no significant abnormalities except for a borderline low Vitamin B12. He told me he usually went to bed at 2 a.m. and woke up at 8 a.m. I recommended that he go to bed before midnight. On our follow-up visit, he acted much calmer and appeared better rested. He told me he had taken my advice and started to go to bed earlier. That *one* change had made a huge difference in how he felt. His fatigue was gone. Going to bed earlier made all the difference. And it didn't require a pill.

I hope this chapter has given you a better understanding of why sleep is so important to your health and well-being and ultimately the world. When you are well rested, you are better equipped to manage your stress and your life. Being calmer and less reactive to others creates a positive ripple effect that could make our society a kinder, gentler, more humane place to be.

Endnotes

1   University of Pennsylvania School of Medicine. "One in four Americans develop insomnia each year: 75 percent of those with insomnia recover." ScienceDaily. www.sciencedaily.com/releases/2018/06/180605154114.htm (accessed October 10, 2020).

2   Williamson AM, Feyer AM. Moderate sleep deprivation produces impairments in cognitive and motor performance equivalent to legally prescribed levels of alcohol intoxication. *Occup Environ Med. 2000;57(10):649-655. doi:10.1136/oem.57.10.649.*

3   Potkin KT, Bunney WE Jr. Sleep improves memory: the effect of sleep on long term memory in early adolescence. *PLoS One. 2012;7(8):e42191. doi:10.1371/journal.pone.0042191.*

4   Staffe AT, Bech MW, Clemmensen SLK, Nielsen HT, Larsen DB, Petersen KK. Total sleep deprivation increases pain sensitivity, impairs conditioned pain modulation and facilitates temporal summation of pain in healthy participants. PLoS One. 2019 Dec 4;14(12):e0225849. doi: 10.1371/journal.pone.0225849. PMID: 31800612; PMCID: PMC6892491.

5   Babson KA, Trainor CD, Feldner MT, Blumenthal H. A test of the effects of acute sleep deprivation on general and specific self-reported anxiety and depressive symptoms: an experimental extension. *J Behav Ther Exp Psychiatry. 2010;41(3):297-303. doi:10.1016/j.jbtep.2010.02.008.*

6   Xiaoyu Li, ScD, Yongmei Liu, MD, PhD, Stephen S Rich, PhD, Jerome I Rotter, MD, Susan Redline, MD, MPH, Tamar Sofer, PhD, 0291 Sleep Disordered Breathing Associated with Epigenetic Age Acceleration: Evidence from the Multi-Ethnic Study of Atherosclerosis, *Sleep, Volume 42, Issue Supplement_1, April 2019, Pages A118–A119, https://doi.org/10.1093/sleep/zsz067.290.*

7   Tosini G, Ferguson I, Tsubota K. Effects of blue light on the circadian system and eye physiology. *Mol Vis. 2016;22:61-72. Published 2016 Jan 24.*

8   Karadag E, Samancioglu S, Ozden D, Bakir E. Effects of aromatherapy on sleep quality and anxiety of patients. Nurs Crit Care. 2017 Mar;22(2):105-112. doi: 10.1111/nicc.12198. Epub 2015 Jul 27. PMID: 26211735.

9   Kuhn E, Weiss BJ, Taylor KL, et al. CBT-I Coach: A Description and Clinician Perceptions of a Mobile App for Cognitive Behavioral Therapy for Insomnia. *J Clin Sleep Med. 2016;12(4):597-606. Published 2016 Apr 15. doi:10.5664/jcsm.5700.*

10   Elsas SM, Rossi DJ, Raber J, et al. Passiflora incarnata L. (Passionflower) extracts elicit GABA currents in hippocampal neurons in vitro, and show anxiogenic and anticonvulsant effects in vivo, varying with extraction method. *Phytomedicine. 2010;17(12):940-949. doi:10.1016/j.phymed.2010.03.002.*

11   Abbasi B, Kimiagar M, Sadeghniiat K, Shirazi MM, Hedayati

M, Rashidkhani B. The effect of magnesium supplementation on primary insomnia in elderly: A double-blind placebo-controlled clinical trial. *J Res Med Sci. 2012;17(12):1161-1169.*

12 Social Laughter Triggers Endogenous Opioid Release in Humans. Sandra Manninen, Lauri Tuominen, Robin I. Dunbar, Tomi Karjalainen, Jussi Hirvonen, Eveliina Arponen, Riitta Hari, Iiro P. Jääskeläinen, Mikko Sams, Lauri Nummenmaa, Journal of Neuroscience 21 June 2017, 37 (25) 6125-6131; DOI: 10.1523/JNEUROSCI.0688-16.2017.

13 Oberbarnscheidt T, Miller NS. The Impact of Cannabidiol on Psychiatric and Medical Conditions. *J Clin Med Res. 2020;12(7):393-403. doi:10.14740/jocmr4159.*

14 Brown JD, Winterstein AG. Potential Adverse Drug Events and Drug-Drug Interactions with Medical and Consumer Cannabidiol (CBD) Use. *J Clin Med. 2019;8(7):989. Published 2019 Jul 8. doi:10.3390/jcm8070989.*

15 https://www.akc.org/expert-advice/lifestyle/should-my-dog-sleep-with-me/.

CHAPTER 5
GAIN CONTROL OF YOUR MIND

"Life is not about how fast you run or how high you climb but how well you bounce."—*Vivian Komori*

BUILDING ON DON'T MESS WITH STRESS™ (DMWS)

As I HAVE BEEN PUTTING the finishing touches on this book over a two-day span, I received news that a dear friend had been diagnosed with breast cancer that possibly spread and a close relative had died suddenly.

That was a lot to take in and absorb in such a short time. Wow!

I had been doing my daily DMWS practices—eating right, meditating, exercising, doing yoga/stretching, and getting to bed early, except when I had to take care of a patient after midnight.

I believe that doing my DMWS helped me stay centered and buffer the stressors that had confronted me.

I still felt the effects of the sudden sad news of my friend and relative, but I found I was better able to deal with it all than if I hadn't been doing these lifestyle measures.

Learning how to manage our minds and thoughts is the linchpin of the **Don't Mess With Stress™** program. Coping with daily stress is hard enough. The ultimate challenge is how best to manage stress when life throws you a curveball so that you maintain your health and well-being in the process.

The goal is to build emotional resilience. Those who are resilient don't just survive but thrive in the face of adversity. You can be one of them.

The greater part of this book is devoted to the **Don't Mess With Stress™ "Core Four"—Diet, Meditation, Walk (move, exercise, dance), and Sleep**, thus creating a solid foundation of physical, emotional, and mental fitness, and resilience. This framework gives you the energy and fortitude to confront your challenges and flourish. The following builds on this structure, providing a roadmap for engaging your mind to navigate stress.

Let's begin by reviewing the facts about mental and emotional resilience, then move on to various strategies you can employ to manage stress, especially the kind that hits you broadside.

SHORING UP YOUR MENTAL AND EMOTIONAL RESILIENCE

Resilience has been described as how quickly you can bounce back from stressful life events. When I was a child, I owned an inflatable plastic clown weighted at the bottom. When you hit it, it would quickly fall to the ground and pop back up. Like the weighted toy clown, resilient people respond better to life's challenges because they have the ability to come back to their center quicker.

Managing your stress by building resilience will require you to employ a few key concepts and tools in addition to the Don't Mess with Stress™ foundation. As you continue to use and practice these tools, you will strengthen not only your mental and emotional fitness[1] but build up your physical resilience as well. Everything is connected: your mind and emotions affect your physical body, and as we have learned in the chapter on Diet, your brain affects your gut and your gut affects your brain. Increasing your mental and emotional resilience will ultimately make you a happier, healthier person— one who can project positive energy out into the world and make it a better place.

Several factors enhance the functioning of your mind and thinking, contributing to healthy stress management and stress hardiness. Here are **5 elements** I believe are key to developing mental and emotional resilience.

These elements are based on the work of Southwick, Vythilingam, and Charney, in their article, "The Psychobiology of Depression and Resilience to Stress: Implications for Prevention and Treatment."[2]

1. A positive mindset
2. Purpose and meaning in life
3. Humor
4. Social connections and nourishing relationships, and
5. Compassion for self and others.

A POSITIVE MINDSET

The first element is to develop a positive and optimistic mindset,[3] a general philosophy of looking at the world within you and without. Cultivating a positive mental attitude and outlook influences your thinking and behavior. However, maintaining that positivity is not always easy, especially when confronting life's challenges. We live in a time of extreme unrest. The news confronts us every minute with the latest acts of terrorism, threats of disease, and dire consequences of political strife. You may ask, "How can I remain positive in the face of such negativity?"

Hard as it might be, our only choice is to find the good in these situations. Becoming **cognitively flexible** helps us to devise novel solutions to new challenges, to reframe and reappraise challenging conditions with a positive slant. By embracing the adversity and leaning in when you want to step back, you increase your ability to cope. This process known as **neuroplasticity** stimulates new connections in the brain. You learn to accept what is and focus on what you can do in a challenging or adverse situation.

FINDING PURPOSE AND MEANING

The second element that helps to improve our mental health is finding purpose and meaning in life. This perspective can come in the form of religion, spirituality, or another philosophy you resonate with. Research shows that religiousness and spirituality[4] are associated with decreased depression in the face of adversity and trauma. Attending services, virtually or in person (once it is safe to do so), at a synagogue, church, temple, or mosque can often help to uplift. There are many variants within the world's faiths to choose from; e.g., from orthodox to reformed. If you were raised in a religion or practice that no longer brings comfort, another denomination might work better for you. Our world offers a wealth of religions. Buddhism might be just what you need to help you focus on the present. Journaling your experiences can also help you in your journey to self-discovery.

You may find spiritual comfort in reading memoirs of other people's spiritual or religious journeys. When I was in college, many of my classmates found comfort in *Zen in the Art of Motorcycle Maintenance*, by Robert M. Pirsig. Earlier generations read with interest the spiritual awakening of the protagonist in Somerset Maugham's *The Razor's Edge*. *The Chronicles of Narnia*, written by British author and lay theologian C.S. Lewis, contains a spiritual—in this case Christian—message. You may prefer to look for answers in *Living a Joyous Life: The True Spirit of Jewish Practice*, by Rabbi David Aaron. For people interested in an eastern philosophy, "*The Autobiography of a Yogi*, by Paramahansa Yogananda, is a classic. A simple internet search will yield many, many more suggestions. Don't forget that your public library and librarians are wonderful resources. If you don't have time to read, download an audiobook you can listen to while you walk or do chores.

Many people also find purpose in contribution. Helping others through charities and civic organizations fosters a sense of well-being and satisfaction that boosts our resilience. Explore your local and global community to see where you can make a positive difference.

Work can also be a source of meaning and fulfillment.

HUMOR

The third element is humor and laughter. Research has shown that using humor and laughter as a tool in stressful situations can interrupt, ameliorate, or lighten the stress response. It can also decrease the risk of depression.[5] Humor and laughter are immune boosters that decrease levels of cortisol, one of the stress hormones.[6] Think how relaxed yet buoyant we feel when we truly laugh.

There has been much research on the benefits of laughter. For example, Dr. Jongeun Yim[7] has described the physiological and psychological effects of laughter. Blood flow increases, stress hormones decrease, and endorphins increase. It also appears to improve mental functioning. Psychologically, it helps reduce stress and anxiety. Laughter does also seem to enhance memory. Personal relationships are improved by laughter when people share a laugh. When one person laughs or get giddy others are often stimulated to join in the laughing chorus.

Laughter affects both the mind and the body. It loosens you up and picks up your mood.

I love to laugh! Reading a funny passage, listening to a talented comedian, or hearing a joke can make me laugh out loud. And reliving these funny moments is good for the body.

Even faking or inducing laughter can produce therapeutic effects.

If you have trouble laughing on your own, try a Laughter Club in person or online or Laughter Yoga.[8] Check this out and start laughing now.

Need cheering up? Watch clips of comedians or

political satire on YouTube. Watch a sitcom you find amusing. Read a funny book or one written by a comedian or humorist you admire.

Social Connections and Nourishing Relationships

The fourth element that increases our mental and emotional fitness is social connections and nourishing relationships.

Because of Covid-19, many people have become socially isolated, creating a different kind of pandemic— one of loneliness and depression. This is extremely harmful. Social isolation has been found to decrease cognitive function—especially in older adults[9]—worsen stress and increase inflammation.[10]

It is critical to maintain and seek social connection. To quote one study, social connection "lowers the stress hormone, cortisol, increases resilience and decreases the risk of developing psychiatric or bodily illness after stressful events."[11]

Consequently, having as many social contacts as possible with friends, family, and acquaintances could help improve your immune system and health. If you are living alone, you can sustain social contact virtually via phone calls, Facetime, Zoom, etc. If you are lucky enough to live with people you love, a simple hug can really help. To reference the old AT&T commercial, you should "reach out and touch someone." Doing so either in person or virtually will not only brighten someone else's day and improve their health and well-being, it will also boost your oxytocin[12] levels and lower your stress hormones., strengthening your immune system.

Living with a pet is also a form of social contact. Just petting or holding an animal will go a long way toward decreasing stress and loneliness. There are biochemical reasons why this is so. The social bonding of human-animal interactions is facilitated by the hormone oxytocin produced in both men and women.

HAVING COMPASSION FOR YOURSELF AND OTHERS

Our fifth element necessary for building resilience is having compassion for ourselves and others.[13] Being kind to yourself and letting yourself off the hook when things don't go your way alleviates stress, depression and anxiety and enhances stronger emotional health and self-esteem.

Part of having self-compassion is reflected in the way we talk to ourselves. Our self-talk can either harm or help us based on what we say. As discussed earlier, the field in psychology called Cognitive Behavioral Therapy (CBT) teaches us to challenge our negative or fearful thoughts, called cognitive distortions. With CBT, we replace the negative commentary with rational and upbeat alternatives. Here's an example of this concept: If you were to fail a test in school, you might then worry that you will flunk out altogether and in so doing, cause your life to turn to shambles. Your mind races into ever more dire predictions, including thoughts that you will never amount to anything. In this example, you have catastrophized the moment with your negative thoughts.

Using CBT, instead of catastrophizing, you would take a pause to gather yourself and then conceive of different, more constructive alternatives. For example, you could say, "Okay, I failed this one test this time, but I know I could have studied more and next time I will give myself ample time do so and ace the test. If I just put in a real effort my life will really shine!"

CBT is one way that people can learn to have self-compassion and be kinder to themselves. There are many resources that can show you how to manage your thoughts including Cognitive Behavioral therapists, articles online, and books.

There is also a relatively new modality that builds on CBT called Dialectical Behavior Therapy (DBT). DBT was created by Dr. Marsha Linehan, a psychologist, in the early 1990s. This technique was originally used to treat people who had what is called a Borderline Personality Disorder. In recent years, it has been found to be effective in treating other psychologic conditions, including depression, eating disorders, self-harm, and substance abuse. Of late, people are using DBT to develop better emotional stability and interpersonal skills, which decrease their overall stress.

An important tenet of this work is what Dr. Linehan calls the "Wise Mind." According to Dr. Linehan, we have an "Emotional Mind" and a "Rational Mind." It is the intersection of these two minds that forms the "Wise Mind" that can help us make more sound and thoughtful decisions. In practice, DBT can be of benefit to virtually anyone seeking to develop better emotional regulation. Learning and using these tools can significantly fortify mental and emotional resilience.

To review, we have discussed the five elements of foundational mental and emotional resilience:

1. A positive mindset
2. Purpose and meaning in life
3. Humor
4. Social connections and nourishing relationships, and
5. Compassion for self and others.

By cultivating these five elements, you will build a strong emotional and mental foundation to prepare you for the difficult stressors that you encounter in life.

"IN THE MOMENT" TECHNIQUES TO MANAGE YOUR STRESS

Once you have incorporated the five elements, you will be better equipped to evaluate and manage a stressful event. Here is a list of what I call "In the Moment" techniques that are a pivotal part of the Don't Mess With Stress™ program. They are designed to calm you down when confronted by a stressful situation, to buffer the negative effects of stress hormones, and prevent harmful consequences to your health.

The goal with these techniques is to make you more mindful and less reactive in the moment. Managing your stress proactively will make you not only more mindful of your thoughts, feelings, and emotions, but also those of other people. It is a win-win experience.

I use these techniques myself. I recommend picking 5 or 6 and listing them in in your smartphone notes or on a small card you keep in your wallet. If you can memorize them, that is even better. Here they are.

1. **Pause and breathe**. When confronted by a stressful situation, stop and take a conscious breath. Make it deep and slow. Allow the exhalation to be longer than the inhalation. You can also count your breaths. Just breathing deeply can interrupt the stress response and calm your

physiology down. If you have privacy, you can also place your hand on your abdomen and feel your belly expand as you inhale and flatten as you exhale. Be careful to breathe slowly so you don't hyperventilate.

2. **Cultivate a "Wise Mind" mindset**. Remember to look at your Emotional Mind and your Rational Mind to come up with a "Wise Mind" viewpoint when dealing with stressful situations. The Emotional Mind is ruled by feelings—anger, anxiety, fear—while the Rational Mind is saying—to borrow from the classic TV show *Dragnet*—"Just the facts, ma'am." Our goal is to combine what we feel *and* what we know.

3. **Say, "I am"…"relaxed."** Take a breath in through your nose and think the words "I am…" as you hold your breath for 3 seconds. As you slowly breathe out through your mouth, think the word "Relaxed." Do this 3 times, or for as long as it takes to calm you down. Again, be sure to keep your breathing slow so you don't hyperventilate.

PLEASE NOTE: IF YOU ARE HAVING CHEST PAIN, CALL YOUR DOCTOR IMMEDIATELY OR CALL 911.

4. **Hold your hand over your heart**. Connect with your body to remind yourself of your mortality.

Put your hand on your heart as you breathe in and out into your heart area. Don't worry about whether it is in through your nose or your mouth. Just focus on your heart.

5. **Be mindful**. Try to be in the present moment without judging what is happening as good or bad. Try to observe it from a calm and compassionate viewpoint.

6. **Use positive self-talk**. Catch yourself before you head down a negative spiral. Ideally, write down three positive traits you possess. For example, "I care about people." "I care about this office." "I am a kind person." Turn the tables on negative harmful thinking. For more on this subject, I recommend Shad Helmstetter's self-help book, *What to Say When You Talk to Your Self*. Experiment until you recognize what it feels like in your body to have a positive thought versus a negative thought. When I have negative thoughts, my body shuts down and feels constricted. I feel almost ill. Have self-compassion, forgive yourself. Self-soothe. Tell yourself you are doing the best you can in this moment, and that this too, shall pass.

7. **Express gratitude**. In the moment of the stressful situation, reflect on something you are grateful for. Expressing gratitude—whether in writing, out loud, or in your thoughts—has been shown to

reduce stress.[14]

8. **Focus on someone or someplace you love**. Think of a beloved pet, friend, grandchild, place—it could be a fantasy land—and feel in your heart the love you have for that person or place.

9. **Do something nice for someone, even a stranger**. Give a compliment, hold the door, smile, pay it forward by paying for the coffee of the person ahead of you in line. Being considerate takes the focus off you and your stress in the moment. Your generosity will make you feel good and decrease those stress hormones.

10. **Listen to music that calms you**. This is an easy recommendation to follow. Research shows that listening to music that relaxes you decreases levels of the stress hormone cortisol.[15]

When you are stressed, immediately activate your first choice "In the Moment" technique. If, after a few minutes, you find it is not working, go to number 2 and so on, until you start feeling relief. The techniques will help you become more centered, thoughtful, and reflective in the moment. Whether you are at the supermarket standing in the 10-item line behind a person with 20 items, are late to work, or are feeling disrespected or overlooked for a job promotion, you need to prevent the stress response from running rampant in your body. The goal is to manage your mind, emotions, and behaviors, and ultimately your health.

I HOPE THIS BOOK HAS given you the insights and tools to build your mental and emotional resilience and has empowered you to respond calmly and rationally to life's challenges. Having a positive mental attitude greatly affects your well-being and the world around you.

It is important that you not allow stress to damage you physically and mentally because the long-term effects can be injurious. I understand that you may find it impossible to incorporate all of these many recommendations. The longest walk begins with one short step. Aim to set realistic goals for each of the areas and try to add to and improve your skill sets.

The result will be a happier, calmer life for you, your loved ones, and everyone you encounter.

Good luck on your journey to a less stressful, more peaceful, and calmer life. Being centered and living in the moment will allow you to be kinder to yourself and others, which will ultimately make the world a better place.

Endnotes
1   Rosenbaum D, Kroczek AM, Hudak J, Rubel J, Maier MJ, Sorg T, Weisbender L, Goldau L, Mennin D, Fresco DM, Fallgatter AJ, Ehlis AC. Neural correlates of mindful emotion regulation in high and low ruminators. Sci Rep. 2020 Sep 24;10(1):15617. doi: 10.1038/s41598-020-71952-5. PMID:

2   Southwick SM, Vythilingam M, Charney DS. The psychobiology of depression and resilience to stress: implications for prevention and treatment. Annu Rev Clin Psychol. 2005;1:255-91. doi: 10.1146/annurev.clinpsy.1.102803.143948. PMID: 17716089.

3   Seligman MEP. Positive Psychology: A Personal History. Annu Rev Clin Psychol. 2019 May 7;15:1-23. doi: 10.1146/annurev-clinpsy-050718-095653. Epub 2018 Dec 10. PMID: 30525996.

4   Cherry KE, Sampson L, Galea S, Marks LD, Stanko KE, Nezat PF, Baudoin KH. Spirituality, Humor, and Resilience After Natural and Technological Disasters. J Nurs Scholarsh. 2018 Sep;50(5):492-501. doi: 10.1111/jnu.12400. Epub 2018 Jul 29. PMID: 30058284.

5   Southwick SM et al. Op. Cit.

6   Rnic K, Dozois DJ, Martin RA. Cognitive Distortions, Humor Styles, and Depression. Eur J Psychol. 2016 Aug 19;12(3):348-62. doi: 10.5964/ejop.v12i3.1118. PMID: 27547253; PMCID: PMC4991044.

7   Therapeutic Benefits of Laughter in Mental Health: A Theoretical Review. JongEun Yim. 2016 Volume 239 Issue 3 Pages 243-249.

8   Laughteryoga.org

9   Dajani DR, Uddin LQ. Demystifying cognitive flexibility: Implications for clinical and developmental neuroscience. *Trends Neurosci.* 2015;38(9):571-578. doi:10.1016/j.tins.2015.07.003

10   https://www.the-scientist.com/features/how-social-isolation-affects-the-brain-67701

11   Ozbay F, Johnson DC, Dimoulas E, Morgan CA, Charney D, Southwick S. Social support and resilience to stress: from neurobiology to clinical practice. Psychiatry (Edgmont). 2007;4(5):35-40.

12   Pohl TT, Young LJ, Bosch OJ. Lost connections: Oxytocin and the neural, physiological, and behavioral consequences of disrupted relationships. *Int J Psychophysiol.* 2019;136:54-63. doi:10.1016/j.ijpsycho.2017.12.011

13   Rosenfeld AJ. The Neuroscience of Happiness and Well-Being: What Brain Findings from Optimism and Compassion Reveal. Child Adolesc Psychiatr Clin N Am. 2019 Apr;28(2):137-146. doi: 10.1016/j.chc.2018.11.002. Epub 2018 Dec 22. PMID: 30832948.

14   Kreitzer MJ, Telke S, Hanson L, Leininger B, Evans R. Outcomes of a Gratitude Practice in an Online Community of Caring. J Altern Complement Med. 2019 Apr;25(4):385-391. doi: 10.1089/

acm.2018.0460. Epub 2019 Feb 20. PMID: 30785803.

15 Linnemann A, Ditzen B, Strahler J, Doerr JM, Nater UM. Music listening as a means of stress reduction in daily life. Psychoneuroendocrinology. 2015 Oct;60:82-90. doi: 10.1016/j.psyneuen.2015.06.008. Epub 2015 Jun 21. PMID: 26142566.

ACKNOWLEDGMENTS

THIS BOOK HAS TAKEN ME over twenty years to write. I have started and stopped so many times, and have written several iterations of drafts. I finally put my foot down and said I had to write it. I had to overcome my perfectionism and fear of "not getting it right."

To support me in getting this book written, I have many people to thank.

First, I want to thank my beloved mother and father. They have always been there for me, believed in me and supported me and my three amazing siblings in whatever we decided to do in our lives. My mother, a former schoolteacher and businesswoman, coined the title, "Don't Mess with Stress." My father, a PhD in Education, an author of Bud's Easy ™ Research Paper Computer Manual and Bud's Easy™ Note Taking System, as well as a former English teacher, school principal, and former superintendent of schools, provided additional editing, helpful comments, and proofreading that really impacted the form of this book. He was indispensable to its production.

My brother James also helped with editing and thoughtful comments, in addition to his steady emotional support.

My sister Caroline, brother-in-law Anthony, and their amazing sons and my nephews, Asher and Emmanuel, provided tremendous support during our quarantining together and have always been there for me.

My brother Rob has also always been there for me. His wife Tracy, my dear sister-in-law, helped me clarify my thinking with regards to the book. And their kids, Noah and Rebecca, have supported me as well.

I want to thank my Aunt Myrna Ezersky, for her love and support.

Claire and Paul Finkel, for their love and support.

Madeline and Steve Anbinder, for their unceasing generosity and love.

Helen and Paul Anbinder, for their support.

My dear friend and colleague, Virginia Darrow-Menegaz, MS, RD, Functional Nutritionist, who kept pushing me over the years to write this book. Thank you, Ginny!

My amazing editor and friend, Catherine Treadgold, who stepped in at a crucial time and made this book happen. Thank you, Cat, for your patience with me. I am sorry if I caused you any stress! You made this book come to life.

Alice Phillips, a dear friend and excellent editor, who worked with me in the early stages.

John Eggen and Christy Tryhus for their publishing wisdom and support early in the process.

Lisa Lewtan for her early and helpful support.

Laura Petersen and Allison Melody for the Copy That Pops method and all of the group of 27 members, especially Aimee Carlson and Tamar Medford!

Fred Travis, PhD, Director, Center for Brain, Consciousness and Cognition, MIU, for his insights and research pertaining to the benefits of Transcendental Meditation.

Mike Potenza, Director of Strength and Conditioning, San Jose Sharks, for his expertise in movement and exercise.

Dr. Nan Lu, OMD, Traditional Chinese Medicine expert and Qi Gong Master, for his insights, especially about sleep.

The late Bruce McEwen, PhD, pioneering neuroscientist in the field of stress research at Rockefeller University, who let me interview him many years ago for this book.

Michelle Ghilotti, for her wisdom, coaching, and counsel.

Mary Solanto, PhD, whose training in organization

and focus empowered me to move forward.

My dear friends and college classmates, Wendy Gerber and Anna Zuckerman Vdovenko for their love and support.

One of my oldest and dearest friends, Lisa Wessan, LICSW, for her wonderful support of me.

My dear friend Barbara Schottenfeld, for always supporting me on this mission.

My good friend, Andrew (Andy) Weinrich, for reading earlier chapters and providing helpful comments.

Richard Burst-Lazarus, for creating my Don't Mess with Stress™ binder with my drafts and for his encouragement during our Skype work sessions.

Christine Loomis for having me speak at the Princeton Club of New York on Don't Mess with Stress™ and for supporting me and my work.

My friend Jenny du Pont, for her support of this book and for sending me pertinent information for the research.

The exceptional attorney Sandra Hudak of Amster Rothstein & Ebenstein LLP for her trademark work.

Barry B. Cepelewicz, MD, Esq., Partner/Director of Garfunkel Wild, for his legal expertise.

Sally Zasloff, Debby Davenport, MD, Joy Sardinsky and the Launchettes, and the women of the Virtual Happy Hour for their support.

Alice Rischert for attending my lectures and for her support and Linsey Tully and Jane Algus, MD, for their all-around support.

Ingrid Tarjan for being an excellent fitness trainer. You taught me a different way to think about exercise.

Connie Bennett, fellow author and friend, for all of her support over the years.

Dan Chayefsky for your love, wisdom, and encouragement, always.

Deborah Hallahan, eternally optimistic and supportive of me and my work.

Judy Benjamin, a force of nature and co-book-writing buddy for her support and wisdom.

Dr. Kristina Pikunas, a new friend and colleague, for her support during our weekly calls.

My dear friends and fellow colleagues, Dr. Claudia Cooke and Dr. Patricia Muehsam, for their healing and loving support.

My awesome neighbor Harriet Moulton for always being there when I needed her.

My dear wonderful friend and prince of a human being Dr. Saul Pressner, Biomimetic dentist extraordinaire, for his enduring love and support.

Ms. Debra Poneman, whose teachings empowered me to move forward.

My amazing Assistant Jasmin Funez for keeping my office running smoothly and for all of her support.

And lastly, my patients, who have entrusted me with their health and who have taught me so much.

Thank you so much for reading Don't Mess With Stress™. If you enjoyed this book and found it useful, please help me spread the word on social media by "liking" my Facebook page, www.facebook.com/Dr-Jill-Baron-274141239291450, and following me on Twitter: @drjillbaronmd.

Also, to get the latest on managing your stress and living a healthy life, sign up for my Health and Well-Being newsletter at www.drjillbaron.com.

Made in the USA
Middletown, DE
20 January 2021